Red

Bury College
Woodbury LR

371.14124
KAM

This book is due for return on or before the last date shown below.

1 9 JAN 2017

2 0 JUN

27 FEB 2018

2 4 SEP 2021

1 6 APR 2018

15 MAY 2023

WITHDRAWN

1 5 MAY 2018

1 6 OCT 2023

4 JUN 2018 0 7 NOV 2023

1 2 JUN 2018

D0625052

Teena K

Te A Ha L

Supporting Teaching and Learning in Schools

HODDER
EDUCATION
AN HACHETTE UK COMPANY

Woodbury Centre

00260237

Orders: please contact Bookpoint Ltd, 130 Milton Park, Abingdon, Oxon OX14 4SB. Telephone: (44) 01235 827720. Fax: (44) 01235 400454. Lines are open from 9.00–5.00, Monday to Saturday, with a 24 hour message answering service. You can also order through our website www.hoddereducation.co.uk

If you have any comments to make about this, or any of our other titles, please send them to educationenquiries@hodder.co.uk

British Library Cataloguing in Publication Data
A catalogue record for this title is available from the British Library

ISBN: 9781444121315

First Edition Published 2010
Impression number   10 9 8 7 6 5 4
Year   2012

Copyright © 2010 Teena Kamen

All rights reserved. No part of this publication may be reproduced or transmitted in any form or by any means, electronic or mechanical, including photocopy, recording, or any information storage and retrieval system, without permission in writing from the publisher or under licence from the Copyright Licensing Agency Limited. Further details of such licences (for reprographic reproduction) may be obtained from the Copyright Licensing Agency Limited, of Saffron House, 6-10 Kirby Street, London EC1N 8TS.

Cover photo © Kiselev Andrey Valerevich /Shutterstock; apple © Ingram Publishing Limited
Typeset by Pantek Arts, Ltd, Maidstone, Kent
Printed in Dubai for Hodder Education, An Hachette UK company,
338 Euston Road, London NW1 3BH

Contents

Dedication

To my son, Tom Jennings, with love and affection

Acknowledgements

Many thanks to the children, families, students and colleagues who I have worked with over the years including: the Marr family and the Pinder family; The Badger's Sett Play Scheme; St. Thomas's Rainbow Guides; Rood End Primary School; Withymoor Primary School; Birmingham College of Food, Tourism & Creative Studies; Sandwell College of FE & HE. Special thanks to Rebecca Brown, Chris Helm, Terry James and Pauline White for their technical support and invaluable contributions during the writing of this book. Teena Kamen

The authors and the publishers would like to thank the following for permission to reproduce material in this book:

p. 23 © Henryk T. Kaiser/Rex Features / p. 24 © Rossario – Fotolia.com / p. 26 © Monkey Business – Fotolia.com / p. 33 © Rob – Fotolia.com / p. 63 © Monkey Business Images/Rex Features / p. 71 © Gideon Mendel/Corbis / p. 84 © Linda Westmore/Education Photos / p. 85 © Big Cheese Photo LLC/Alamy / p. 94 © Monkey Business – Fotolia / p. 105 © Rob – Fotolia.com / p. 120 © Zakharov Evgeniy – Fotolia.com / p. 122 © Tim OLeary/Corbis / p. 133 © Monkey Business Images/Rex Features / p. 142 © Monkey Business Images/Rex Features / p. 148 © Nicole Hill/Rubberball/Corbis / p. 158 © imagebroker/Alamy / p. 164 © Action Press/Rex Features / p. 167 © Olga Chernetskaya – Fotolia.com / p. 169 © OJO Images/Rex Features / p. 171 © Thomas Barwick/Dgital Vision/Getty Images / p. 182 © arabianEye/Corbis / p. 184 Sally and Richard Greenhill © Sally Greenhill / p. 186 © www.purestockX.com / p. 191 © Yellow Dog Productions/ Image Bank/Getty Images / p. 193 © Jose Luis Pelaez, Inc./Blend Images/Corbis / p. 202 © Brian Mitchell/ Photofusion / p. 207 © Burger/ phanie/Rex Features / p. 214 EAT FIT poster © Comic Company 2010 / p. 216 © Cultura / Alamy / p. 217 © Superstudio/ Image Bank/Getty Images / p. 229 © OJO Images Ltd/Alamy

Every effort has been made to obtain necessary permission with reference to copyright material. The publishers apologise if, inadvertently, any sources remain unacknowledged and will be glad to make the necessary arrangements at the earliest opportunity.

Introduction

Teaching Assistant's Handbook for Level 2 is a comprehensive and practical guide to supporting the development and learning of pupils in a variety of educational settings including primary, secondary and special schools as well as extended schools.

The book covers practical considerations such as:

- supporting the teacher in the delivery of learning activities
- maintaining pupil safety and security
- supporting positive behaviour
- supporting assessment and record keeping
- using ICT to support teaching and learning
- developing effective practice
- supporting pupils with special educational needs.

The book clearly links theory and practice by exploring different theoretical aspects of children's development (e.g. social, physical, intellectual, communication and emotional) and relating these to providing practical support for teaching and learning in schools. The book explains complex theoretical issues in ways which can be easily understood, but is sufficiently challenging to assist students in developing a sound knowledge-base to complement their practical skills.

This book is for students (and their tutors/assessors) on teaching assistant courses and provides the background knowledge relevant to the requirements of supporting teaching and learning in primary, secondary and special schools.

How to use this book

This book contains the knowledge requirements for a range of topics related to supporting the development and learning of pupils. The book includes practical ideas for linking knowledge and understanding with performance criteria to meet the National Occupational Standards (NOS) in Supporting Teaching and Learning in Schools for Level 2.

The book is suitable for students (and their tutors) on a range of courses for school support staff on the new Qualifications and Credit Framework (QCF) for Supporting Teaching and Learning in Schools (STLS) being implemented from September 2010:

- Level 2 Award in Support Work in Schools
- Level 2 Certificate in Supporting Teaching and Learning in Schools
- Level 2 Certificate in Supporting the Wider Curriculum in Schools.

The headings in each section are related to NOS in Supporting Teaching and Learning in Schools for Level 2 for ease of reference – you can access the specifications, 'National occupational standards for supporting teaching and learning in schools', via the Training and Development Agency for Schools (TDA) website, **www.tda.gov.uk**.

Read the relevant chapter for the Unit(s) you are currently studying and do the activities as specified. The Key Tasks (which are linked to the NOS in Supporting Teaching and Learning in Schools for Level 2) can be done in any order, as appropriate to your training provider's and/or setting's requirements, and may contribute to your formal assessment. However, it is suggested that you read Chapter 1: **Supporting child and young person development** *before* you start planning play and learning activities for pupils. *Do* remember to follow your setting and/or centre guidelines. You need only complete the Key Tasks relevant to the units you are studying and/or your role and responsibilities in school.

Principles and values

All work within the setting should be underpinned by the principles and values as stated in the National Occupational Standards in Children's Care, Learning and Development.

Principles:
1. The welfare of the child is paramount.
2. Practitioners contribute to children's care, education and learning, and this is reflected in every aspect of practice and service provision.
3. Practitioners work with parents and families who are partners in the care, development and learning of their children and are the child's first and most enduring educators.

Values:
1. The needs, rights and views of the child are the centre of all practice and provision.
2. Individuality, difference and diversity are equally valued and celebrated.
3. Equality of opportunity and anti-discriminatory practice are actively promoted.
4. Children's health and well-being are actively promoted.
5. Children's personal and physical safety is safeguarded whilst allowing for risk and challenge as appropriate to the capabilities of the child.
6. Self-esteem, resilience and positive self-image are recognised as essential to every child's development.
7. Confidentiality and agreements about confidential information are respected as appropriate unless a child's protection and well-being is at stake.
8. Professional knowledge, skills and values are shared appropriately in order to enrich the experience of children more widely.
9. Best practice requires reflection and a continuous search for improvement.

(NDNA, 2004)

1. Supporting child and young person development

This chapter relates to QCF unit:

TDA 2.1 Child and young person development

Observing children's development

Accurate observations and assessments are essential to effective educational practice. Careful observations enable you and the teacher to make objective assessments relating to each pupil's: behaviour patterns; learning styles; levels of development; existing skills; curriculum strengths and weaknesses; current learning needs and learning achievements. Assessment of this information can help highlight and celebrate pupils' strengths as well as identify any gaps in their learning. This information can form the basis for the ongoing planning of appropriate learning activities; it may also be a useful starting point for future learning goals or objectives.

The purpose of observation

There are many reasons why it is important to observe pupils. For example:

- to understand the wide range of skills in all areas of their development
- to know and understand the sequences of development
- to use this knowledge to link theory with your own practice in the school
- to assess development and existing skills or behaviour
- to plan activities appropriate to individual learning needs.

You will usually be observing activities which are part of the pupil's usual routine. You can observe pupils' development, learning and behaviour in a variety of situations. For example, you might observe the following situations:

- A child talking with another child or adult.
- An adult working with a small group of children or young people.
- A child or a small group of children playing indoors or outdoors, or participating in a small or large group discussion, e.g. circle time.
- An adult reading/telling a story to a child or group of children.
- A child or group of children participating in a creative, literacy, mathematics or science activity, e.g. doing painting, writing, numeracy work or carrying out an experiment.

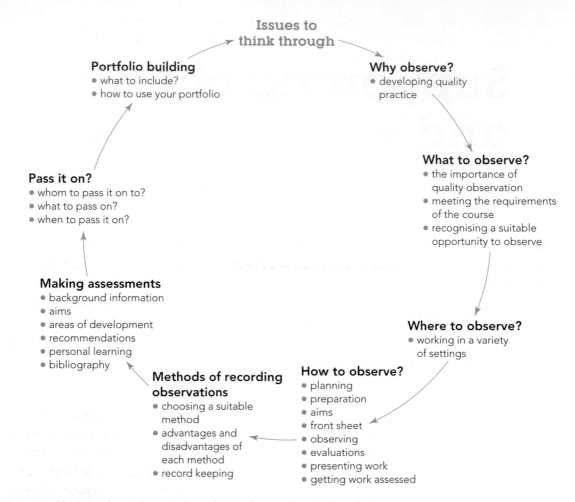

Figure 1.1: *Thinking About Observing* by Jackie Harding and Liz Meldon-Smith

 **Activity!**

Write a short account explaining the importance and purpose of observing and assessing pupils' development.

The basic principles of child observation

Some important points have already been mentioned with regard to observing children's development, learning and behaviour. You also need to consider the following:

1. **Confidentiality must be kept at all times**. You must have the senior practitioner's and/or the parents' permission before making formal observations of children. (See details below.)

2. **Be objective**. You should not jump to premature conclusions. Only record what you actually see or hear not what you think or feel. For example, the statement 'The child cried' is objective, but to say 'The child is sad' is subjective, as you do not know what the child is feeling; children can cry for a variety of reasons, e.g. to draw attention to themselves or to show discomfort.

3. **Remember equal opportunities**. Consider children's cultural backgrounds, e.g. children may be very competent at communicating in their community language, but may have

more difficulty in expressing themselves in English; this does not mean they are behind in their language development. Consider how any special needs may affect children's development, learning and/or behaviour.

4. **Be positive!** Focus on the children's strengths not just on any learning or behavioural difficulties they may have. Look at what children can do in terms of their development and/or learning and use this as the foundation for providing future activities.

5. **Use a holistic approach.** Remember to look at the 'whole' child. You need to look at all areas of children's development in relation to the particular aspect of development or learning you are focusing on.

6. **Consider the children's feelings.** Depending on the children's ages, needs and abilities, you should discuss the observation with the children to be observed and respond appropriately to their views.

7. **Minimise distractions.** Observe children without intruding or causing unnecessary stress. Try to keep your distance where possible, but be close enough to hear the children's language. Try not to interact with the children (unless it is a participant observation – see below), but if they do address you be polite and respond positively, e.g. explain to the children simply what you are doing and keep your answers short.

8. **Practise!** The best way to develop your skills at observing children's development, learning and behaviour is to do observations on a regular basis.

Confidentiality

The teacher and your college tutor/assessor will give you guidelines for the methods most appropriate to your role in your particular school. Your observations and assessments must be in line with the school's policy for record keeping and relevant to the routines and activities of the pupils you work with. You must follow the school's policy regarding confidentiality at all times and be able to implement data protection procedures as appropriate to your role and responsibilities. (See sections on confidentiality matters in Chapter 3 and maintaining pupil records in Chapter 14.)

The school should obtain permission from the parents or carers of the pupils being observed, e.g. a letter requesting permission to do regular observations and assessments could be sent out for the parents to sign giving their consent. If you are a student, before doing any tasks for your assessment involving observations of children you MUST negotiate with the class teacher when it will be possible for you to carry out your observations and have written permission to do so.

In Practice

Jamie is working as a teaching assistant with pupils aged 6 to 7 years. During a learning activity Jamie observes that one of the pupils is very quiet and withdrawn which is unusual behaviour for this particular child. What would you do in this situation? Who would you report your concerns to?

Observation methods

When observing pupils you need to use an appropriate method of observation as directed by the teacher. When assisting the teacher in observing and reporting on a pupil's development ensure that you consider all relevant aspects of development, for example: Social; Physical; Intellectual; Communication and Emotional. These can easily be remembered using the mnemonic **SPICE**.

You may observe an individual pupil or group of pupils on several occasions on different days of the week and at different times of the day. Use developmental charts for the pupil's age group to identify areas of development where the pupil is making progress, as well as those where the pupil is underachieving. For example, a pupil with limited speech may still be developing positive social relationships with other children by using non-verbal communication during play activities.

Observations and assessments should cover all relevant aspects of development including: physical skills; language and communication skills; social and emotional behaviour during different activities. You may be able to assist the teacher to compile a portfolio of relevant information about each pupil. A portfolio could include: observations; examples of the children's work; checklists of the children's progress. Assessment of this information can help highlight and celebrate the pupil's strengths as well as identify any gaps in their learning. This information can form the basis for the ongoing planning of appropriate learning activities and be a useful starting point for future learning goals/objectives. (Information about formative and summative assessments is in Chapter 14.)

Recording observations and assessments

You should record your observations and assessments using an agreed format. This might be a: written descriptive account; structured profile (with specified headings for each section); pre-coded system of recording. Once you have recorded your observation of the pupil (or group of pupils), you need to make an assessment of this information in relation to:

🔑 **key words**

Assessment: the evaluation of a pupil's development and learning.

- The aims of the observation e.g. why you were doing this observation
- What you observed about the pupil's development, learning and/or behaviour in *this* particular activity
- How this compares to the expected level of development for a pupil of this age
- Any factors which may have affected the pupil's ability to learn and/or behave, e.g. the immediate environment, significant events, illness, pupil's cultural background, special needs.

Your assessment may include charts, diagrams and other representations of the data you collected from your observation (see examples of observation charts opposite). Your college tutor or assessor should give you guidelines on how to present your observations. Otherwise you might find the suggested format on page 6 useful:

Tick chart: *Group observations of children at snack/meal time*

Self-help skills	Children's names			
	Shafik	Sukhvinder	Ruth	Tom
goes to the toilet				
washes hands				
dries hands				
chooses own snack/meal				
uses fingers				
uses spoon				
uses fork				
uses knife				
holds cup with 2 hands				
holds cup with 1 hand				

KEY: ✓ = competent at skill.   \ = attempts skill/needs adult direction.   ✗ = no attempt/requires assistance.

Pie chart: *Time sample observation of child's play activities*

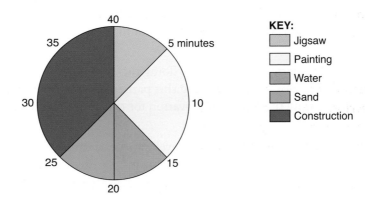

Bar graph: *Time sample observation of child's social play*

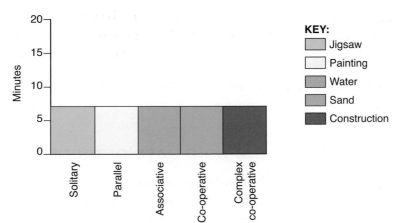

Figure 1.2: Observation charts

Suggested format for recording observations

Number/title of observation:
Date of observation:
Method: e.g. naturalistic, structured, snapshot, longitudinal, time sample, event sample, participant, non-participant, target child, trail or movement, checklist, coded observation or diary.
Start time:
Finish time:
Number of pupils/staff:
Permission for observation: e.g. teacher
Type of setting and age range: e.g. primary school, secondary school, special school.
Immediate context/background information: including the activity and its location.
Description of pupil(s): including age(s) in years and months.
Aims: why are you doing this particular observation?
Observation: the actual observation e.g. free description, pie chart, bar graph or tick chart.
Assessment: include the following • Did you achieve your aims? • Comparison of the pupil's development with the expected development of a pupil of this age, looking at all aspects of the pupil's development but with particular emphasis on the focus area (e.g. physical, social and emotional or communication and intellectual skills) • References to support your comments.
Personal learning: what you gained from doing this observation, e.g. what you have learned about this aspect of development and using this particular method of observing pupils e.g. was this the most appropriate method of observation for this type of activity?
Recommendations: • On how to encourage/extend the pupil's development, learning and/or behaviour in the focus area, e.g. suggestions for activities to develop the pupil's literacy or numeracy skills. • For any aspect of the pupil's development, learning and/or behaviour which you think requires further observation and assessment.
References/bibliography: list details of all the books used to complete your assessment.

 **Activity!**

Find out what your school's policies are regarding pupil observations and assessments, confidentiality and record keeping and data protection procedures.
Keep this information in mind when doing your own observations of pupils.

Planning provision to promote development

As directed by the teacher you may be involved in planning provision for the pupils you work with based on assessments of their developmental progress. You should recognise that developmental progress depends on each pupil's level of maturation and their prior experiences. You should take these into account and have realistic expectations when planning activities to promote pupils' development. This includes regularly reviewing and updating plans for individual pupils and ensuring that plans balance the needs of individual pupils and the group as appropriate to your school. You should know and understand that pupils develop at widely different rates but in broadly the same sequence. When planning provision to promote pupils' development you need to recognise that children's development is holistic even though it is divided into different areas e.g. **S**ocial; **P**hysical; **I**ntellectual; **C**ommunication and language and **E**motional. Remember to look at the 'whole' child, e.g. you need to look at *all* areas of children's development in relation to the particular aspect of development or learning you are focusing on when planning provision to promote pupils' development.

The planning cycle

Following observations and assessments of a pupil's development, learning and/or behaviour, the recommendations can provide the basis for planning appropriate activities to encourage and extend the pupil's skills in specific areas. Effective planning is based on individual needs, abilities and interests, hence the importance of accurate and reliable child observations and assessments. You will also support the teacher in planning provision based on the requirements for the relevant curriculum frameworks.

When planning learning activities, your overall aims should be to: support the development and learning of *all* the pupils you work with; ensure every pupil has full access to the appropriate curriculum; meet pupils' individual developmental and learning needs and build on each pupil's existing knowledge, understanding and skills. (For detailed information on planning learning activities see Chapter 7.)

Implementing and evaluating plans to promote development

Good preparation and organisation are essential when implementing plans to promote pupils' development including: having any instructions and/or questions for the pupil or group of pupils ready, e.g. prompt cards, worksheet, work card or written on the board; ensuring sufficient materials and equipment including any specialist equipment and setting out the materials and equipment on the table ready or letting the pupils get the resources out for themselves depending on their ages and abilities. Implementing an activity may involve: giving out any instructions to the pupils; showing pupils what to do, e.g. demonstrate a new technique; keeping an individual pupil and/or group of pupils on task; clarifying meaning and/or ideas; explaining any difficult words to the pupils; assisting pupils with any special equipment, e.g. hearing aid or a Dictaphone; providing any other appropriate assistance; encouraging the pupils to tidy up afterwards as appropriate to the ages and abilities and remembering to maintain pupil safety at all times.

After you have planned and/or implemented an activity you will need to evaluate it. Some evaluation also occurs during the activity, providing continuous assessment of a pupil's performance. It is important to evaluate the activity so that you can: assess whether the activity has been successful, e.g. the aims and objectives have been met; identify possible ways in which the activity might be modified/adapted to meet the individual needs of the pupil or pupils and provide accurate information for the teacher, SENCO or other professionals about the successfulness of a particular activity. The teacher or your college tutor/assessor should give you guidelines on how to present your activity plans. If not, you might find this suggested format useful:

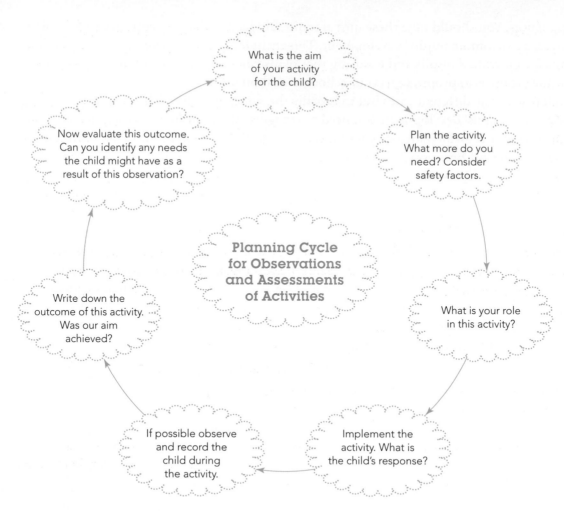

Figure 1.3: *Planning children's activities* by Jackie Harding and Liz Meldon-Smith

The figure shows a "Planning Cycle for Observations and Assessments of Activities" with the following steps:

- What is the aim of your activity for the child?
- Plan the activity. What more do you need? Consider safety factors.
- What is your role in this activity?
- Implement the activity. What is the child's response?
- If possible observe and record the child during the activity.
- Write down the outcome of this activity. Was our aim achieved?
- Now evaluate this outcome. Can you identify any needs the child might have as a result of this observation?

Suggested format for planning activities

Title: brief description of the activity.
Date and time: the date and time of the activity.
Plan duration: how long will the activity last?
Aim and rationale: the main purpose of the activity including how it will encourage development, learning and/or behaviour. The rationale should outline why this particular activity has been selected (e.g. identified particular pupil's need through observation; links to topics/themes within the group, class or setting). How does the activity link with any curriculum requirements?
Staff and setting: the roles and number of staff involved in the activity plus the type of setting and the age range of the setting.
Details of the pupils(s): activity plans involving an individual pupil or small group of pupils should specify first name, age in years and months plus any relevant special needs; activity plans involving larger groups should specify the age range and ability levels.
Learning objectives for the pupil(s): indicate what the child or children could gain from participating in the activity in each developmental area: **SPICE**.

Preparation: what do you need to prepare in advance (e.g. selecting or making appropriate materials; checking availability of equipment)? Think about the instructions and/or questions for the pupil(s); will these be spoken and/or written down, e.g. on a worksheet/card or on the board? Do you need prompt cards for instructions or questions?

Resources: what materials and equipment will you need? Where will you get them from? Are there any special requirements? Remember equal opportunities including special needs. How will you set out the necessary resources (e.g. setting out on the table ready or the pupils getting materials and equipment out for themselves)?

Organisation: where will you implement the activity? How will you organise the activity? How will you give out any instructions the pupils need? Will you work with pupils one at a time or as a group? Are there any particular safety requirements? How will you organise any tidying up after the activity? Will the pupils be encouraged to help tidy up?

Implementation: describe what happened when you implemented the activity with the pupil(s). Include any alterations to the original plan, e.g. changes in timing or resources.

Equal opportunities: indicate any multicultural aspects to the activity and any additional considerations for pupils with special needs.

Review and evaluation: review and evaluate the following:
- The aims and learning outcomes/objectives
- The effectiveness of your preparation, organisation and implementation
- What you learned about development and learning
- What you learned about planning activities
- Possible modifications for future similar activities.

References and/or bibliography: the review and evaluation may include references appropriate to development, learning and behaviour. Include a bibliography of any books used as references or for ideas when planning the activity.

 **Activity!**

Describe how *you* help to plan, implement and evaluate activities to promote pupils' development in your school. Include examples of any planning sheets you use.

Understanding child and young person development

When supporting child and young person development, it is essential to always look at the 'whole' child or young person. This means looking at *all* areas of their development in relation to the particular aspect of development or learning you are focusing on. We therefore refer to child and young person development as holistic with each area being interconnected. For example, when observing a pupil's writing skills as well as looking at their intellectual development you will need to consider the pupil's:

 key words

Holistic: looking at the 'whole' child or young person, e.g. all aspects of the child or young person's development.

- physical development (fine motor skills when using a pencil or pen)
- language development and communication skills (vocabulary and structure of language used during their writing)
- social and emotional development (interaction with others and behaviour during the writing activity).

The basic patterns of child and young person development

It is more accurate to think in terms of <u>sequences</u> of children and young people's development rather than <u>stages</u> of development. This is because stages refer to development that occurs at *fixed ages* while sequences indicates development that follows the same basic pattern *but not necessarily at fixed ages.* You should really use the term 'sequences' when referring to all aspects of development. However, the work of people such as Mary Sheridan provides a useful guide to the <u>milestones</u> of *expected* development, that is, the usual patterns of development or <u>norm</u>. As well as their chronological age, children and young people's development is affected by many other factors, e.g. maturation, social interaction, play opportunities, early learning experiences and special needs. The developmental charts below *do* indicate specific ages, but only to provide a framework to help you understand the basic patterns of development. *Always remember that all children and young people are unique individuals and develop at their own rate.*

key words

Milestones: significant skills which are developed in and around certain ages as part of the usual or expected pattern of development.

Norm: the usual pattern or expected level of development/behaviour.

Sequences: development following the same basic patterns but not necessarily at fixed ages.

Stages: development which occurs at fixed ages.

Egocentric: pre-occupied with own needs; unable to see another person's viewpoint.

 Activity!

- What are the principles of child and young person development?
- Describe the basic patterns of development.

The sequences of development 0 to 16 years

The sequence of children's development for each age range is divided into five different aspects:

* **S**ocial * **P**hysical * **I**ntellectual * **C**ommunication and language * **E**motional.

The Sequence of Children's Development: 0 to 3 Months

Social Development

- Cries to communicate needs to others; stops crying to listen to others.
- Responds to smiles from others; responds positively to others e.g. family members and even friendly strangers unless very upset (when only main caregiver will do!).
- Considers others only in relation to satisfying own needs for food, drink, warmth, sleep, comfort and reassurance.

Physical Development

- Sleeps much of the time and grows fast.
- Tries to lift head.
- Starts to kick legs with movements gradually becoming smoother.
- Starts to wave arms about.
- Begins to hold objects when placed in hand e.g. an appropriate size/shaped rattle.
- Grasp reflex diminishes as hand and eye coordination begins to develop.
- Enjoys finger play, e.g. simple finger rhymes.
- Becomes more alert when awake.
- Learns to roll from side on to back.
- Sees best at distance of 25 cm then gradually starts watching objects further away.
- Needs opportunities to play and exercise e.g. soft toys, cloth books and play-mat with different textures and sounds.

Intellectual Development

- Recognises parents; concentrates on familiar voices rather than unfamiliar ones.
- Aware of different smells.
- Explores by putting objects in mouth.
- Observes objects that move; responds to bright colours and bold images.
- Stores and recalls information through images.
- Sees everything in relation to self (is **egocentric**).

Communication and Language Development

- Recognises familiar voices; stops crying when hears them.
- Aware of other sounds; turns head towards sounds.
- Responds to smiles; moves whole body in response to sound/to attract attention.
- Pauses to listen to others; makes noises as well as crying, e.g. *burbling*.

Emotional Development

- Becomes very attached to parent/carer (usually the mother).
- Experiences extreme emotions, e.g. very scared, very happy or very angry; these moods change in an instant.
- Requires the security and reassurance of familiar routines.
- May be upset by unfamiliar methods of handling and care.

The Sequence of Children's Development: 3 to 9 Months

Social Development

- Responds positively to others, especially to familiar people such as family members; by 9 months is very wary of strangers.
- Communicates with others by making noises and participating in 'conversation-like' exchanges; responds to own name.
- Begins to see self as separate from others.

Physical Development

- Establishes head control; moves head round to follow people and objects.
- Begins to sit with support; from about 6 months sits unsupported.
- Rolls over.
- May begin to crawl, stand and cruise while holding on to furniture (from about 6 months).
- Learns to pull self up to sitting position.
- Begins to use palmar grasp and transfers objects from one hand to the other.
- Develops pincer grasp using thumb and index finger from about 6 months.
- Continues to enjoy finger rhymes.
- Drops things deliberately and searches for hidden/dropped objects (from about 8 months).
- Puts objects into containers and takes them out.
- Enjoys water play in the bath.
- Needs opportunities for play and exercise including soft toys, board books, bricks, containers, activity centres, etc.

Intellectual Development

- Knows individuals and recognises familiar faces.
- Recognises certain sounds and objects.
- Shows interest in everything especially toys and books.
- Concentrates on well-defined objects and follows direction of moving object.
- Anticipates familiar actions and enjoys games such as 'peep-po'.
- Searches for hidden or dropped objects (from about 8 months).
- Observes what happens at home and when out and about.
- Explores immediate environment once mobile.
- Processes information through images.
- Enjoys water play in the bath.
- Sees everything in relation to self (is still egocentric).

Communication and Language Development

- Responds with smiles.
- Recognises family names, but cannot say them.
- Enjoys looking at pictures and books.
- Even more responsive to voices and music.
- Participates in simple games e.g. 'peep-po'; tries to imitate sounds e.g. during rhymes.
- Starts *babbling*, uses single syllable sounds e.g. 'daa', 'baa' and 'maa'.
- From about 7 months uses two syllable sounds e.g. 'daada', 'baaba', 'maama'
- Shouts to attract attention.

Emotional Development

- Has strong attachment to parent/carer (usually the mother).
- Develops other attachments to people sees regularly.
- By 6 or 7 months shows clear preferences for familiar adults as can differentiate between individuals.
- Demonstrates strong emotions through body language, gestures and facial expressions.
- Dislikes anger in others and becomes distressed by it.
- Has clear likes and dislikes, e.g. will push away food, drink or toys does not want.

The Sequence of Children's Development: 9 to 18 Months

Social Development

- Responds to simple instructions (if wants to!).
- Communicates using (limited) range of recognisable words.
- Shows egocentric behaviour e.g. expects to be considered *first*; *all* toys belong to them.
- Is unintentionally aggressive to other children.

Physical Development

- Is now very mobile e.g. crawls, bottom-shuffles, cruises, walks.
- Starts to go upstairs (with supervision) but has difficulty coming down.
- Needs safe environment in which to explore as becomes increasingly mobile e.g. remember safety gates on stairs, etc.
- Throws toys deliberately.
- Watches ball rolling towards self and tries to push it back.
- Has mature pincer grasp and can scribble with crayons.
- Points to objects using index finger.
- Places one (or more) bricks on top of each other to make a small tower.
- Holds a cup and tries to feed self.
- Continues to enjoy finger rhymes plus action songs.
- Needs space, materials and opportunities to play alongside other children.

Intellectual Development

- Explores immediate environment using senses, especially sight and touch; has no sense of danger.
- Concentrates more, due to curiosity and increased physical skills, but still has short attention-span.
- Follows one-step instructions and/or gestured commands.
- Observes other people closely and tries to imitate their actions.
- Uses 'trial and error' methods when playing with bricks, containers.
- Searches for hidden or dropped objects (aware of object permanence).
- Learns that objects can be grouped together.
- Continues to store and recall information through images.
- Is still egocentric.

Communication and Language Development

- Continues to imitate sounds; starts *jargoning* e.g. joins up syllables so more like 'sentences' such as 'Maama-baaba-daa'.
- Learns to say first real words, usually the names of animals and every day things.
- Uses gestures to emphasise word meanings.
- Uses vocabulary of between 3 and 20 words.
- Participates in simple finger rhymes; continues to enjoy books.
- Over-extends words, that is uses same word to identify similar objects e.g. *all* round objects are called 'ball'.

Emotional Development

- Likes to get own way; gets very angry when adult says 'No!'.
- Has emotional outbursts ('temper tantrums') when does not get own way or is otherwise frustrated, e.g. unable to do activity because of physical limitations.
- Shows fear in new situations, e.g. attending parent/toddler group, visiting somewhere new such as the farm or nature centre.
- Relies on parent/carer for reassurance and support in new situations.
- Is upset by the distress of other children (even if they caused it).
- Seeks reassurance and contact with familiar adults throughout waking hours.

Communication and Language Development

- Has vocabulary of about 300 words.
- Uses more adult forms of speech, e.g. sentences now include words like that, this, here, there, then, but, and.
- Can name main body parts.
- Uses adjectives, e.g. big, small, tall; words referring to relationships, e.g. I, my, you, yours.
- Asks questions to gain more information.
- Sings songs and rhymes; continues to participate in action songs and enjoy books/stories.
- Can deliver simple messages.

Emotional Development

- May still rely on parent/carer for reassurance in new situations or when with strangers.
- Still experiences emotional outbursts as independence grows and frustration at own limitations continues, e.g. aggressive towards toys that cannot get to work.
- Begins to understand the feelings of others but own feelings are still the most important.
- Has very limited understanding of other people's pain, e.g. if hits another child.
- Feels curious about their environment but has no sense of danger, e.g. that they or other people can be hurt by their actions.

The Sequence of Children's Development: 3 to 5 Years

Social Development

- Enjoys the company of others; learns to play *with* other children, not just alongside them.
- Uses language to communicate more and more effectively with others.
- Develops self-help skills (e.g. dressing self, going to the toilet) as becomes more competent and confident in own abilities.
- Still wants to please and seeks approval from adults.
- Observes closely how others behave and imitates them.
- Still fairly egocentric; may get angry with other children if disrupt play activities or snatch play items required for own play; expects adults to take *their* side in any dispute.
- Gradually is able to share group possessions at playgroup or nursery.

Physical Development

- Usually clean and dry but may have occasional 'accidents'.
- Able to run well – and stop!
- Competent at gross motor skills such as jumping, riding a tricycle, climbing play apparatus, using a swing.
- Throws and catches a ball but is still inaccurate.
- Fine motor skills continue to improve, e.g. can use scissors.
- Continues to enjoy action songs plus simple singing and dancing games.
- Needs space, materials and opportunities to play cooperatively with other children.

Intellectual Development

- Learns about basic concepts through play.
- Experiments with colour, shape and texture.
- Recalls a simple sequence of events.
- Follows two or three-step instructions including positional ones, e.g. 'Please put your ball in the box under the table'.
- Continues to enjoy imaginative and creative play.
- Interested in more complex construction activities.
- Concentrates on more complex activities as attention-span increases.
- Plays cooperatively with other children; able to accept and share ideas in group activities.
- Shows some awareness of right and wrong, the needs of others.
- Holds strong opinions about likes and dislikes.
- Processes information using language.

Communication and Language Development

- Has vocabulary of between 900 and 1500 words.
- Asks lots of questions.
- Uses language to ask for assistance.
- Talks constantly to people known well.
- Gives very simple accounts of past events.
- Can say names of colours.
- Begins to vocalise ideas.
- Continues to enjoy books, stories, songs and rhymes.
- Listens to and can follow simple instructions; can deliver verbal messages.

Emotional Development

- Less reliant on parent/carer for reassurance in new situations.
- May be jealous of adult attention given to younger sibling or other children in a group.
- Argues with other children but is quick to forgive and forget.
- Has limited awareness of the feelings and needs of others.
- May be quite caring towards others who are distressed.
- Begins to use language to express feelings and wishes.
- Still have emotional outbursts especially when tired, stressed or frustrated.

The Sequence of Children's Development: 5 to 7 Years

Social Development

- Enjoys the company of other children; may have special friend(s).
- Uses language even more effectively to communicate, share ideas, engage in more complex play activities.
- Appears confident and competent in own abilities.
- Cooperates with others, takes turns and begins to follow rules in games.
- Seeks adult approval; will even blame others for own mistakes to escape disapproval.
- Observes how others behave and will imitate them; has a particular role model.
- May copy unwanted behaviour, e.g. swearing, biting or kicking to gain adult attention.

Intellectual Development

- Learns to read more complex texts and continues to develop writing skills.
- Enjoys number work, but may still need real objects to help mathematical processes.
- Enjoys experimenting with materials and exploring the environment.
- Develops creative abilities as coordination improves, e.g. more detailed drawings.
- Begins to know the difference between real and imaginary, but still enjoys imaginative play.
- Interested in more complex construction activities.
- Has longer attention span; does not like to be disturbed during play activities.
- Follows increasingly complex instructions.
- Enjoys board games and other games with rules; also computer games.
- Develops a competitive streak.
- Has increased awareness of right and wrong, the needs of others.
- Sees other people's points of view.
- Seeks information from various sources, e.g. encyclopaedia, Internet.
- Processes expanding knowledge and information through language.

Communication and Language Development

- Has extensive vocabulary of between 4000 and 10,000 words.
- Uses more complex sentence structures.
- Develops more complex reading and writing skills including improved comprehension, more accurate spelling, punctuation and joined-up writing.
- Continues to enjoy books, stories and poetry.
- Gives very detailed accounts of past events and can anticipate *future* events.
- Vocalises ideas and feelings in more depth.
- Listens to and follows more complex instructions.
- Appreciates jokes due to more sophisticated language knowledge.
- Uses literacy skills to communicate and to access information, e.g. story and letter writing, use of dictionaries, encyclopaedia, computers, Internet, e-mail.

Emotional Development

- Becomes less egocentric as understands feelings, needs and rights of others.
- Still wants things that belong solely to them, e.g. very possessive of own toys.
- Becomes more aware of own achievements in relation to others but this can lead to a sense of failure if feels does not measure up; hates to lose.
- May be very competitive; rivalry may lead to aggressive behaviour.
- Argues with other children but may take even longer to forgive and forget.
- Aware of wider environment, e.g. weather, plants, animals, and people in other countries.

The Sequence of Children's Development: 12 to 16 Years

Social Development

- Continues to enjoy the company of other children/young people; individual friendships are still important; belonging to group or gang becomes increasingly important.
- The desire for peer approval can overtake the need for adult approval and may cause challenges to adult authority at home, school or in the setting particularly in teenage years.
- Participates in team games/sports or other group activities including clubs and hobbies.
- May be strongly influenced by role models in media, e.g. sports celebrities, film/pop stars.
- Communicates effectively and uses language to resolve difficulties in social interactions.
- Can be very supportive towards others experiencing difficulties at home or school, etc.

Physical Development

- Can dress/undress self including intricate fastenings and shoelaces.
- Grows taller and thinner; continues losing baby teeth, physical changes of puberty.
- Enjoys team games and sports.
- Rides a bicycle with competence and confidence.
- Improved fine motor skills makes handwriting easier and more legible.
- Can do more complex construction activities.
- Enjoys singing and dancing but performs set dance routines instead of dancing games.
- Needs space, materials and opportunities to play cooperatively with other children.

Intellectual Development

- Reads more complex texts with improved comprehension and extends writing skills.
- Understands more abstract mathematical/scientific processes, e.g. algebra, physics.
- Develops more creative abilities, e.g. very detailed drawings and stories.
- Knows the difference between real and imaginary.
- Has increased concentration levels and continues to follow more complex instructions.
- Continues to enjoy board games and computer games which require strategy skills.
- Has well-defined understanding of right and wrong; can consider the needs of others.
- Sees other people's point of view.
- Continues to seek information from various sources, e.g. encyclopaedia, Internet.
- Continues to process increasing knowledge and information through language.

Communication and Language Development

- Has an extensive and varied vocabulary of between 10,000 and 20,000 words.
- Uses appropriate language styles for different occasions, e.g. standard English.
- Has more complex reading skills including detailed comprehension skills.
- Writing skills include accurate spelling and punctuation; neat and legible joined-up writing.
- Can use different writing styles including word-processing on a computer.
- Continues to enjoy more complex texts including fiction, poetry and factual books.
- Gives very detailed accounts of past events using varied expression and vocabulary.
- Can anticipate future events and give detailed reasons for possible outcomes.
- Vocalises ideas and feelings in greater depth including justifying own views and opinions.
- Listens to and follows complex sets of instructions; appreciates complex jokes/word play.
- Continues to use literacy skills to communicate and to access information, e.g. taking notes, writing essays/letters; using dictionaries/thesaurus, encyclopaedia; computers, Internet, e-mail.

Emotional Development

- Sensitive to own feelings and those of others with a growing understanding of the possible causes for why people feel and act as they do.
- Emotional changes due to puberty.
- Understands issues relating to fairness and justice.
- Can anticipate people's reactions and consider the consequences of own actions.
- Is increasingly able to see different viewpoints to resolve difficulties in relationships.
- Has confidence in own skills/ideas; able to be assertive rather than aggressive or passive.
- May have very strong opinions or beliefs, leading to arguments with adults and peers; may hold grudges and find it difficult to forgive or forget.
- Has more understanding of complex issues, e.g. ethics, philosophy, religion, politics.

- Describe the different aspects of development (e.g. **SPICE**).
- Outline the sequences of development for the age group you currently work with.

Supporting social development

Children and young people's social development involves developing social skills as part of the socialisation process. The socialisation process involves the development of:

- acceptable behaviour patterns
- self-control and discipline
- independence (including self-help skills e.g. feeding, toileting, dressing, etc.)
- awareness of self in relation to others
- positive relationships with others
- understanding the needs and rights of others
- moral concepts (e.g. understanding the difference between right and wrong).

Socialisation determines how children relate socially and emotionally to others. Children need to learn how to deal appropriately with a range of people, situations and emotions. An essential aspect of socialisation is encouraging children to behave in socially acceptable ways. Children model their attitudes and actions on the behaviour of others. They imitate the actions and speech of those they are closest to e.g. acting at being 'mum', 'dad' or 'teacher'; copying the actions and mannerisms of adults around the home, child care setting or school.

All adults working with children need to be aware of the significant impact they make to children's social (and emotional) development by providing positive role models. When working with children you should strike a balance between allowing for the children's increasing need for independence and providing adequate supervision with appropriate guidelines for socially acceptable behaviour. (For detailed information about supporting positive behaviour see Chapter 8.)

key words

Behaviour: a person's actions, reactions and treatment of others.
Role models: significant people whose actions, speech or mannerisms are imitated by a child or young person.
Socialisation: how children relate socially and emotionally to other people.

 Key Task

Observe a group of pupils during a play activity or playing a game. Focus on one pupil's social development. In your assessment comment on:

- the pupil's level of social interaction
- the pupil's use of language and communication skills
- the pupil's behaviour during the activity
- the role of the adult in promoting the pupil's social development
- suggestions for further activities to encourage or extend the pupil's social development including appropriate resources.

NOS Links:

Level 2:   STL 2.2   STL 9.1   STL 9.2   STL 10.1

Figure 1.4: Children playing a game

Five ways to promote children's social development

As a teaching assistant, you should support the teacher in providing appropriate routines and activities to encourage and extend the children's social skills. You can help to promote children's social development by:

1. **Setting goals and boundaries** to encourage socially acceptable behaviour as appropriate to the children's ages and levels of development. Using appropriate praise and rewards can help.

2. **Encouraging the children's self-help skills.** Be patient and provide time for the child to do things independently, e.g. choosing play activities and selecting own materials; helping to tidy up and dressing independently during dressing-up.

3. **Providing opportunities for the children to participate in social play**, e.g. encourage children to join in team games, sports and other cooperative activities.

4. **Using books, stories, puppets and play people** to help the children understand ideas about fairness, jealousy and growing up and dealing with conflict situations.

5. **Encouraging the children to take turns**, e.g. sharing toys and other play equipment. Emphasising cooperation and sharing rather than competition.

Key Task

- Plan a play activity which encourages or extends a pupil's social development. For example, encouraging the pupil to use a variety of social skills such as: demonstrating positive behaviour; being independent (e.g. using self-help skills or making choices); using effective communication skills; sharing resources; understanding the needs and feelings of others.
- Use the assessment from your previous observation of a pupil's social development as the basis for your planning.
- If possible, ask the class teacher for permission to implement the activity. Evaluate the activity afterwards.

NOS Links:

Level 2: STL 1.2 STL 1.3 STL 2.4 STL 10.1

Supporting physical development

As young children grow they go through striking changes in body shape and features from helpless baby to wobbly toddler to physically competent 4 year old. At birth a baby's head accounts for about 25 per cent of the full body length. During childhood a child's head grows the least compared to the growth of the rest of the body. By adulthood the head is about 12 per cent of body. After the changes of early childhood, the next major changes occur in puberty as girls start becoming mature females and boys start becoming mature males. (Lindon, 2007)

As children grow up, their bodies are affected by what they eat and drink as well as how bodies are used. Imbalanced diets and inappropriate exercise all affect children's physical development. Healthy eating and exercise habits should be established in childhood which can then be maintained into adulthood. (Lindon, 2007)

As well as growth, physical development also involves children's increasing ability to perform more complex physical activities involving gross motor skills, fine motor skills and coordination.

<u>Gross motor skills</u> involve whole body movements. Examples of gross motor skills include walking, running, climbing stairs, hopping, jumping, skipping, cycling, swimming, climbing play apparatus, playing badminton, basketball, football, hockey, netball, rugby or tennis. Children need strength, stamina and suppleness to become proficient in activities involving gross motor skills.

<u>Fine motor skills</u> involve whole hand movements, wrist action or delicate procedures using the fingers, e.g. the palmar grasp (grabbing and holding a small brick), the pincer grip (using the thumb and index finger to pick up a pea) and the tripod grasp (holding a crayon, pencil or pen). Examples of fine motor skills include drawing, painting, writing, model-making, playing with wooden/plastic bricks or construction kits, cutting with scissors, doing/undoing buttons, shoelaces and other fastenings. Children need good concentration levels and hand–eye coordination (see below) to become proficient in activities involving fine motor skills.

<u>Coordination</u> involves hand–eye coordination, whole body coordination and balance. Examples of hand–eye coordination include drawing, painting, using scissors, writing and threading beads. Examples of whole body coordination include crawling, walking,

key words

Coordination: action involving the organised use of muscles for movement e.g. walking (whole body coordination), drawing (hand–eye coordination) and hopping (balance).

Fine motor skills: action involving whole hand movements, wrist action or delicate procedures using the fingers.

Gross motor skills: action involving whole body movements such as large muscle movement, body control and coordination.

Figure 1.5: Children playing on a swing

cycling, swimming and playing football or netball. Examples of balance include hopping and gymnastics. Coordination plays an important part in developing children's gross and fine motor skills. Coordination and balance are needed to improve children's gross motor skills.

You should provide appropriate play and learning activities for children to develop their physical skills. Remember that some children may be limited in their physical abilities due to physical disability, sensory impairment or other special needs.

 Key Task

Observe a pupil involved in a physical activity, e.g. using play equipment or PE apparatus. Focus on the physical skills demonstrated by the pupil. In your assessment comment on:

- the pupil's gross motor skills
- the pupil's fine motor skills
- the pupil's coordination skills
- the role of the adult in promoting the pupil's physical development
- suggestions for further activities to encourage or extend the pupil's physical development.

NOS Links:

Level 2:   **STL 2.1**   **STL 2.2**   **STL 2.3**   **STL 2.4**   **STL 9.1**   **STL 9.2**

Five ways to promote children's physical development

As a teaching assistant, you should support the teacher in promoting children's physical development and physical well-being. You can help to promote children's physical development by:

1. **Providing play opportunities for children to explore and experiment** with their gross motor skills both indoors and outdoors, with and without play apparatus or other equipment. Helping children to practise fine motor skills (e.g. bricks, jigsaws, play dough, sand, construction kits, drawing) and to develop body awareness through action songs such as 'Head, shoulders, knees and toes'.

2. **Maintaining the children's safety** by supervising the children at all times and checking any equipment used meets required safety standards and is positioned on an appropriate surface. Ensure the children know how to use any equipment correctly and safely.

3. **Selecting activities, tools and materials** that are appropriate to the ages and levels of development of the children to help the children practise their physical skills. Encourage children to persevere with tackling new skills that are particularly difficult and praising the children as they become competent in each physical skill.

4. **Using everyday routines** to develop the children's fine motor skills, e.g. getting dressed, dealing with fastenings and shoelaces, using a cup, using a spoon, fork or knife, helping prepare or serve food, setting the table, washing up. (Remember safety.)

5. **Allowing the children to be as independent** as possible when developing their physical skills including adapting activities and/or using specialist equipment for children with special needs to enable their participation in physical activities as appropriate.

- Plan an activity which encourages or extends a pupil's physical skills such as gross motor skills, fine motor skills and/or coordination skills.
- Use the assessment information from your previous observation of a pupil's physical development as the basis for your planning.
- If possible, ask the class teacher for permission to implement the activity. Evaluate the activity afterwards.

NOS Links:

Level 2:   STL 1.1   STL 1.2   STL 1.3   STL 2.1   STL 2.4   STL 10.4

Supporting intellectual development

Intellectual development involves the processes of gaining, storing, recalling and using information. To develop as healthy, considerate and intelligent human beings, all children require intellectual stimulation as well as physical care and emotional security. Children are constantly thinking and learning, gathering new information and formulating new ideas about themselves, other people and the world around them.

The interrelated components of intellectual development are:

- perception
- thinking
- language
- problem-solving
- concepts
- memory
- concentration
- creativity.

Figure 1.6: Adult supporting pupils during a learning activity

Perception involves the ability to identify the differences between objects or sounds. There are two types of perception: *auditory* – differentiating between sounds; *visual* – differentiating between objects or the distance between objects. Children use their senses to explore the objects and sounds in the world around them.

Thinking can be defined as the intellectual process of using information to find solutions. We cannot see a person's thoughts because the thinking process is internal. We can see the process and progress of a person's thinking through their actions and communications. Children can develop their thinking skills through a wide range of learning activities including: problem-solving in mathematics; investigating and hypothesising in science and identifying and solving design needs in technology.

 key words

Perception: using the senses to explore, interpret and organise information in the world around us.

Thinking: the intellectual process of using information to find solutions.

Language is an essential component of intellectual development as it enables children to: make sense of the world around them; access new experiences and store new information; make better connections between existing and new information; develop understanding of concepts (see below); communicate more effectively with others, e.g. ask appropriate questions; verbalise their thoughts and express their opinions and ideas.

Problem-solving involves using the intellectual processes of *logic* and *reasoning* to make personal judgements and making connections between existing information and new information. Children use their existing knowledge and past experiences to solve problems. Children often supplement their lack of knowledge or experience by experimenting, i.e. using a process of trial and error. Making mistakes is part of the learning process. By using logic, children can make reasonable assumptions or predictions about what might happen in a particular situation or to a particular object. Logical thinking and problem-solving skills are essential to making mathematical calculations and scientific discoveries.

Concepts are the ways in which people make sense of and organise the information in the world around them. Concepts can be divided into two categories: *concrete* (e.g. colour, number and shape recognition) and *abstract* (e.g. telling the time). Younger children take longer to understand abstract concepts, but this depends on their individual learning experiences including opportunities to develop a firm understanding of concrete concepts through 'real life' situations. For example, many children do understand the ideas concerning fairness and the rights of people (and animals) to live in freedom if these concepts are linked with real events.

Memory involves the ability to recall or retrieve information stored in the mind. The other intellectual processes would be of little use to children without effective memory skills. Memory skills involve: *recalling information* about past experiences, events, actions or feelings; *recognising information* and making connections with previous experiences and *predicting*, e.g. using past information to anticipate future events. Many intellectual processes involve all three of these memory skills, e.g. problem-solving in mathematics and science or the decoding and comprehension skills needed for reading.

 key words

Concentration: the ability to pay attention to the situation or task in hand.

Concepts: the ways people make sense of and organise information in the world around them.

Creativity: the ability to produce something new through the use of imagination.

Language: the process of using a recognised system of symbols to communicate needs, feelings and thoughts including listening, speaking, reading, writing and non-verbal communication.

Memory: the ability to recall or retrieve information stored in the mind.

Problem-solving: activities which involve finding solutions to a difficulty or question.

Concentration involves the ability to pay attention to the situation or task in hand. A person's concentration level or attention span is the length of time they are able to focus on a particular activity. Some children can concentrate for quite a long time, while other children find their attention starts to wander after just a few minutes. Concentration is a key intellectual skill, which is necessary for the development of other intellectual processes such as language skills and understanding concepts.

Creativity is the use of the imagination. Using the imagination involves the ability to invent ideas or form images of things which are not actually there or do not exist. Children can develop their creative skills in a wide variety of learning activities including: play; art, design and technology; music, dance and drama and stories and poems.

(There is detailed information about how children learn in Chapter 7.)

Key Task

Observe a pupil during a learning activity. Focus on the pupil's intellectual development. In your assessment comment on:

- the pupil's imaginative and creative skills
- the pupil's level of concentration
- any problem-solving skills used by the pupil
- the pupil's use of language and communication skills
- the role of the adult in promoting the pupil's intellectual development
- suggestions for further activities to encourage or extend the pupil's intellectual development including appropriate resources.

NOS Links:

Level 2:   STL 2.1   STL 2.2   STL 2.3   STL 2.4   STL 9.1   STL 9.2

Five ways to promote children's intellectual development

As a teaching assistant, you should support the teacher in providing learning opportunities to encourage children's intellectual skills. You can help to promote children's intellectual development by:

1. **Providing opportunities and materials to increase the children's curiosity**, e.g. books, games, posters, pictures, play equipment and toys. Encourage children to observe details in the environment, e.g. colours, shapes, smells and textures. Talk about weather conditions. Take the children on outings. Do gardening and/or keep pets.

2. **Participating in the children's activities to extend their development and learning** by asking questions, providing answers and demonstrating possible ways to use play equipment and other learning resources. Demonstrate how things work or fit together when the children are not sure what to do. Make sure your help is wanted (and necessary). Use verbal prompts where possible to encourage children to solve the problem for themselves.

3. **Providing gradually more challenging play and learning activities** but do not push the children too hard by providing activities which are obviously too complex; instead of extending the children's abilities this will only put them off due to the frustration of not being able to do the activity. Provide repetition by encouraging the children to play with toys and games more then once; each time they play, they will discover different things about these activities. Encourage acceptable risk taking during play opportunities.

4. **Helping the children to develop their concentration and memory skills by:** ensuring the children are *looking* and *listening* attentively when giving new information; explaining how new information is connected to the children's existing experiences and knowledge (e.g. by linking activities with a common theme); dividing complex activities into smaller tasks to make it easier for children to concentrate; using memory games to encourage/extend concentration levels; singing songs and rhymes, e.g. following a number sequence in songs like *Five brown teddies, Ten green bottles, When I was one I was just begun...*

5. **Encouraging the children to use their senses to experiment with different materials and to explore their environment**, e.g. doing arts and crafts; playing with sand, water, clay, dough and wood; playing with manufactured materials such as plastic construction kits; modelling with safe household junk materials; cooking activities; singing rhymes and songs; clapping games; outings to the local park; matching games, jigsaws and lotto.

Key Task

- Plan a learning activity which encourages or extends a pupil's intellectual development such as: imaginative and creative skills; concentration and memory skills; problem-solving skills; language and communication skills.
- Use the assessment information from your previous observation of a child's intellectual development as the basis for your planning.
- If possible, ask the class teacher for permission to implement the activity. Evaluate the activity afterwards.

NOS Links:

Level 2: STL 1.1   STL 1.2   STL 1.3   STL 2.2   STL 2.3   STL 2.4   STL 10.1
STL 10.2   STL 10.3   STL 10.5   and depending on the learning activity:
STL 7.2   STL 8.2 (ICT)   STL 6.1 (literacy)   STL 6.2 (numeracy)

Supporting communication and language development

Effective communication is made possible through the use and understanding of a shared language system. We communicate because we need to interact with others. Humans are social animals and desire the company of others. We use language as the most effective means of communicating with other people. Language is the **key factor** in all aspects of children's development as it opens the door to all aspects of the human experience:

- communicating with others
- relating to others
- exploring the environment
- understanding concepts
- formulating ideas
- expressing feelings.

The human ability to use language depends on the use of *recognised systems of symbols* and a common understanding of what those symbols mean. Obviously there are many other systems of symbols as indicated by the many different languages and alphabet systems throughout the world. At first, babies and young children are not able to use this complex language system; it takes time for them to learn the system for their particular home or **community language**. Children (and adults) use a variety of different ways to communicate.

The **modes of language** are essential to being able to communicate effectively with others and to being fully involved in a wide range of social interactions. The different modes of language are non-verbal communication, listening, speaking, thinking, reading and writing.

Each mode of language involves a variety of skills that are interrelated; that is some of the skills are required in more than one mode, e.g. listening and speaking both involve oral language while reading and writing both involve written language.

key words

Community language: main language spoken in a child's home.

Key factor: an essential aspect affecting learning and development.

Modes of language: non-verbal communication; listening; speaking; thinking; reading; writing.

Key Task

- Plan an activity which encourages or extends a pupil's language and communication skills. Include a variety of communication techniques such as: active listening (e.g. listening carefully and focus on what the pupil has to say); leaving time for the pupil to respond/talk; careful phrasing of adult questions and responses.
- Use the assessment information from your previous observation of a pupil's language and communication skills as the basis for your planning.
- Consider how you could meet the needs of bilingual children with this activity (see Chapter 11).
- If possible, ask the class teacher for permission to implement the activity. Evaluate the activity afterwards.

NOS Links:

Level 2: STL 1.1   STL 1.2   STL 1.3   STL 2.3   STL 2.4   STL 4.1   STL 4.3
                    STL 10.1   STL 11.2

Supporting emotional development

Emotional development can be defined as the development of personality and temperament. This includes how each child: develops as a unique individual; sees and feels about themselves; *thinks* other people see them; expresses their individual needs, desires and feelings; relates to others and interacts with their environment.

Children inherit their particular temperaments which are then influenced by the environment they are raised in. Babies develop an awareness of others in relation to themselves, e.g. people who fulfil their needs for food and drink, warmth and shelter, sleep, physical comfort and entertainment.

 key words

Personality: distinctive and individual characteristics which affect each person's view of themselves, their needs, feelings and relationships with others.

Temperament: person's disposition or personality especially their emotional responses.

Babies develop strong attachments to the people they see most often and who satisfy the above needs. One attachment is usually stronger than the others and this is usually the baby's mother, but the attachment can be to another family member or anyone outside the immediate family who spends a significant amount of time with the young child such as a grandparent or nanny. The security of these early attachments is essential to babies and young children because they provide a firm foundation for promoting emotional well-being, positive relationships with other people and confidence in exploring the environment. These early attachments enable children to feel secure about their relationships and to develop trust in others. Security and trust are important elements in the young children's ability to separate from their parents and carers in order to develop their own independence and ideas. Another essential aspect of promoting children's emotional development is helping children to recognise and deal with their own feelings and those of other people. (See section on encouraging pupils to recognise and deal with feelings in Chapter 3.)

Another essential aspect of emotional development is self-esteem which involves: feelings and thoughts about oneself (positive or negative); respect or regard for self (or lack of it); consideration of self; self-image (i.e. perception of self) and self-worth (i.e. value of self). The development of self-image and identity are strongly linked to self-esteem. Self-image and identity can be defined as: the individual's view of their own personality and abilities; the individual's perception of how other people view them and their abilities. This involves recognising: ourselves as separate individuals; we are unique individuals with characteristics and abilities that make us separate and different from others; the factors that influence how we identify with other people (e.g. culture, race, etc.) as part of our own identity. (See information about equality, diversity and inclusion in Chapter 4.)

key words

Identity: the characteristics and abilities that make us separate and different from others; the factors that influence how we identify with other people (e.g. culture, race, etc.) as part of our own identity.

Self-image: the individual's view of their own personality and abilities; the individual's perception of how other people view them and their abilities.

Self-esteem: thoughts and feelings about oneself including self-respect, self-worth and self-image.

Key Task

Observe a pupil during an imaginative play or creative activity. Focus on the pupil's emotional development. In your assessment comment on:

- the pupil's imaginative and creative skills
- the pupil's ability to make choices or decisions
- the pupil's use of language to express needs and/or feelings
- the role of the adult in promoting the pupil's emotional development
- suggestions for further activities to encourage or extend the pupil's emotional development including appropriate resources.

NOS Links:

Level 2: STL 2.2   STL 2.3   STL 2.4
          STL 9.1   STL 9.2

Figure 1.8: Child involved in role play

Five ways to promote children's emotional development

As a teaching assistant, you should support the teacher in providing appropriate routines and activities to promote children's emotional development. You can help to promote children's emotional development by:

1. **Using praise and encouragement** to help the pupils focus on what they are good at. Treat every pupil in the school as an individual. Each pupil has unique abilities and needs. Help pupils to maximise their individual potential.

2. **Taking an interest in the pupils' efforts as well as achievements**. Remember the way pupils participate in activities is more important than the end results, e.g. sharing resources, helping others and contributing ideas. Encourage the pupils to measure any achievements by comparing these to their *own* efforts. Foster cooperation between pupils rather than competition.

3. **Giving pupils opportunities to make decisions and choices**. Letting pupils participate in decision-making, even in a small way, helps them to feel positive and important; it also prepares them for making appropriate judgements and sensible decisions later on.

4. **Promote equal opportunities by providing positive images of children and adults** through: sharing books and stories about real-life situations showing children (and adults) the pupils can identify with; providing opportunities for imaginative play that encourage the pupils to explore different roles in positive ways e.g. dressing-up clothes, cooking utensils, dolls and puppets.

5. **Being consistent about rules and discipline**. All pupils need consistency and a clearly structured framework for behaviour so that they know what is expected of them. Remember to label the behaviour not the pupils as this is less damaging to their emotional well-being, e.g. 'That was an unkind thing to say' rather than 'You are unkind'.

 Key Task

- Plan an activity which encourages or extends a pupil's emotional development. For example, encouraging the pupil to use a variety of emotional abilities such as: imaginative and/or creative skills to express feelings; ability to make choices or decisions; language and communication skills to express needs and/or feelings; understanding the needs and feelings of others.

- Use the assessment information from your previous observation of a pupil's emotional development as the basis for your planning.

- If possible, ask the class teacher for permission to implement the activity. Evaluate the activity afterwards.

NOS Links:

Level 2: **STL 1.1**   **STL 1.2**   **STL 1.3**   **STL 2.2**   **STL 2.4**   **STL 10.1**   **STL 10.2**   **STL 10.3**

Identifying transitions

Transitions are central to children's experiences and wellbeing. Transitions can be defined as '... *key events and/or processes occurring at specific periods or turning points during the life course.*' (Vogler et al, 2008; p.1) Transitions are generally linked to changes in a person's appearance, activity, status, roles and relationships as well as changes of setting. (Vogler et al, 2008)

The process of adjusting to a new situation is known as a transition. Transitions involve the experiences of change, separation and loss. A transition may involve the transfer from one setting to another or changes within the same setting. For example: home to childminder's home, nursery, playgroup or school; one year group or Key Stage to another e.g. Reception to Year 1, Key Stage 1 to 2; mainstream to or from special school; secondary school to college or work; staff changes due to illness, maternity leave, promotion, retirement, etc.

 **key words**

Transition: the process of adjusting to a new situation which may involve transfer from one setting to another or changes within the same setting.

Common transitions

The progression from childhood through adolescence to adulthood necessarily involves change. All children and young people will experience some changes in their daily lives as part of growing up. Some changes can be foreseen, or even planned. These changes involve common transitions such as: progressing from one level of development to another e.g. puberty, entering adulthood; starting nursery or school; moving schools e.g. primary to secondary; moving class; starting college or training; entering voluntary or paid work; first sexual experiences.

 **Activity!**

- Identify the common transitions that you have experienced in childhood and adolescence.
- Predict transitions which you are likely to or have experienced in adulthood.

Personal transitions

Transitions may also involve other significant changes in the child's life which may be unforeseen or only happen to some individuals. These changes involve personal or particular transitions such as: death or serious illness of a family member or close friend; parental separation or divorce; moving house; going into hospital; living with disability; death of a favourite pet; arrival of a new baby or step-brothers and sisters; changes in main carer e.g. adoption, fostering, entering / leaving care system; the process of asylum.

 **Activity!**

- Identify your own personal transitions e.g. moving house.
- Describe your emotions and the challenges you faced.
- How did you manage the change?

Family circumstances

There are a number of family circumstances that may lead to particular or personal transition including: birth of sibling; moving house; poverty; environment; employment status; family break-up or divorce; parent's new partner/relationships; terminal illness or death in the family; child abuse and neglect; mental health needs; substance abuse; consequences of crime e.g. parent in prison.

 **Activity!**

Discuss family circumstances which may lead to transition. For example, discuss transition issues from the 'soap operas' or 'real life' shows on television e.g. family break-up or divorce.

How transitions may affect children's behaviour and development

When change unsettles children, their feelings will emerge one way or another. Different patterns of behaviour show how children are trying to cope with change. Children's responses to change are not always negative and some children will go to tremendous lengths to hide their true feelings about certain changes.

Change is not always disruptive or distressing. A lot depends on the emotional competence of the adults and their willingness to find out from the children how they feel about the change instead of assuming everything is okay or expecting turmoil. When facing change, everyone experiences some feelings of confusion and uncertainty. The prospective change may be anticipated with a mixture of emotions such as excitement at a new opportunity, regret for what is being left behind, or elation at leaving an unhappy setting. Change is more likely to cause emotional distress when someone's life has been turned upside down especially by events that could not be anticipated by anyone. The emotions experienced are still unpredictable, for example, anger, sadness, grief, numbness or a combination of these. High levels of distress and disrupted patterns of behaviour or development are more likely when children are not kept informed, feel out of control or cannot access emotional support. Children can feel overwhelmed when more than one significant change occurs during the same period, or when changes keep piling up and there is no prospect of stability. (Lindon, 2007; p.89) For example, children may feel particularly distressed if they are starting school at the same time as moving house and dealing with the arrival of a new baby.

Children may react to change in the following ways:

- They may behave differently from the child you have come to know well. Some children may become quieter and withdraw. Some may show obvious distress or a lowered ability to deal with the usual ups and downs of life in the setting. Depending on your relationship with a child, they may need no more than a friendly or relatively private, 'Is something bothering you?' and the body language that says clearly that you are ready to listen.
- Some children may struggle with emotional distress which then emerges as anger directed at peers or adults who 'deserve' a verbal or physical attack. You need to deal fairly with the outburst and any consequences, but also give the child the chance to talk about what happened soon after the incident. For example, 'I know you shouted at Damian because of the offside business but you were really angry. It looked to me like there's something else weighing you down. What's up?'
- Sometimes children will temporarily regress in their development and self-help skills. It may be that a usually competent child, struck by anxiety, really wants to be cosseted or is keen to say, 'I can't do that'. Children who were dry at night may start to wet the bed, and their distress at this situation can lead them to feel even more emotionally fragile.
- Some children really want to talk – perhaps to a trusted adult. Perhaps you even hear from the child about their dad being made redundant before the parents tell you.
- Depending on the family situation, some children find it harder to say goodbye to their parent when being left at the setting and they may worry about their wellbeing while they are apart.
- Sometimes children demonstrate their concerns through play or they may be unwilling to play as usual. For some children the issues emerge through their drawings or written stories and poems.

(Lindon, 2007; pp.90/91)

The positive and negative effects of transitions

Transition is a natural process and there are often positive effects. For example: increased levels of motivation; promoting development; educational progress; confidence; good health; improved self-esteem; increased independence; ability to form relationships. Successful transitions can lead to a positive self-image (including gender, sexuality and cultural identity) and result in emotionally healthy and resilient children, young people and adults (Turnbull, 2006).

Most transitions that children make are successful, but for a few children they are not. For example: decreased levels of motivation; developmental delay; educational delay; depression; ill health; poor self-esteem; sleep disruption; self-harm; eating disorders; bullied or bullying; dependence; inability to form or sustain relationships; using illegal substances. Unsuccessful transitions have negative implications for their future well-being and their ability to enjoy and achieve in their childhood and adolescence (Turnbull, 2006).

Starting nursery or primary school

Many children (especially young children) experience anxiety and stress when they first attend a new setting or have a new child carer due to:

- Separation from their parent or previous child carer
- Encountering unfamiliar children who may have already established friendships
- The length of time spent in the setting e.g. 8.00am to 6.00pm in a day nursery or 9.00am to 3.30pm in school
- Differences in culture and language of the setting to child's previous experiences
- Unfamiliar routines and rules
- Worry about doing the wrong thing
- Unfamiliar activities such as sports/PE, playtime, lunch time or even story time
- The unfamiliar physical environment which may seem overwhelming and scary
- Difficulties in following more structured activities and adult directions
- Concentrating on activities for longer than previously used to.

Moving from primary to secondary school

Children face a wide range of new experiences when making the transition from primary to secondary school. For example: going from being the oldest to the youngest in their school; moving around for lessons far more; having several subject teachers instead of one class teacher; starting to learn new subjects; being given increased amounts of homework; facing the developmental changes of puberty at the same time. For most children the transition is a smooth one, but some children find it difficult and problematic. (Turnbull, 2006; p.9)

The transition from primary to secondary may cause additional concerns due to:

- Lack of sufficient information about individual children on transfer
- Discontinuity of Year 6 and 7 curriculum despite the National Curriculum
- Decrease in pupil performance after transfer.

Changing schools

If a family moves home, children can change to a new school at any age. These non-compulsory school moves may have important implications for the life chances of the children involved. A study found that: pupils, at all stages of schooling, from lower social background are more likely to switch schools than other pupils; pupils who change schools are more likely to have a low previous academic attainment record than pupils who do not change schools; pupils placed in schools with high Key Stage performance levels move less than pupils from lower performance schools; pupils who move school and home simultaneously are typically more socially disadvantaged than otherwise. This suggests that for many in this group of children there is a potential negative impact on future academic attainment and therefore on these young people's future contribution to society. (Turnbull, 2006; p. 17)

Activity!

- Investigate the effects of starting primary/secondary school or changing schools.
- Consider why some children start primary/secondary school or changing schools with apparently no effects or with a positive response whilst others are distressed.

Support transitions

The *Common Core of Skills and Knowledge for the Children's Workforce* includes children's transitions as a key area of work. In the chapter 'Supporting Transitions', it notes:

As recognised in effective communication and child development, it is important to understand a child or young person in the context of their life, to recognise and understand the impact of any transitions they may be going through. It is also vital to recognise the role of parents and carers in supporting children at points of transition and to understand the need for reassurance, advice and support that parents and carers may express at these points. (DfES, 2005a; p.16)

To alleviate some of this anxiety and stress, preparation is now seen as an essential part of successful transfers and transitions including nurseries, schools, foster care and hospitals. Most settings have established procedures for preparing children for transfers and transitions.

Ten principles to support children's transitions

The National Children's Bureau has developed ten principles to help workers support children and young people's transitions at all ages and whatever the transitions they are facing. These are:

1. Identify key changes, critical moments and transition points for children and young people.

2. Ensure mainstream work with children and young people builds life skills including emotional resilience and empathy, and emphasises the importance of asking for help and support when they are needed.

3. Develop curriculum and project work that focuses on transitions.

4. Prepare children and young people for leaving school or leaving care well in advance, providing an opportunity to reflect on successes and challenges and celebrate their work together.

5. Identify individuals who may need particular support through transitions. Identify the support mechanisms and agencies that are available for the child and their family. Work in partnership to provide this support, where possible.

6. Involve children and young people in providing support to their peers as part of everyday friendships and relationships.

7. Involve and support parents and carers in transitions work.

8. Encourage optimism and work with the excitement and opportunities, as well as the fears and anxieties.

9. If the behaviour of a child or young person changes, encourage them to acknowledge it and talk about it.

10. Provide consistent responses to critical moments and events in children and young people's lives, such as when they are bullied, bereaved or experiencing parental divorce or separation. Ensure the child is at the heart of deciding what support and help they need.

(Worthy, 2005 as quoted in Turnbull, 2006; p.30)

Transitions and children aged 3 to 11 years

The move to nursery or primary school is still a big step, even though many young children have already spent time in other early years group settings such as day nurseries and pre-school playgroups. The first days and weeks are much easier when children have already met their new (next) teacher, who has ideally already visited the children in their current setting as well as welcoming them to the new setting. (Lindon, 2007)

You can help prepare children aged 3 to 11 years for transitions by:
- Talking to the children and explaining what is going to happen
- Listening to the children and reassuring them that it will be fine
- Reading relevant books, stories and poems about transitions e.g. starting nursery or primary school; moving to secondary school; visiting the dentist; going into hospital
- Watching appropriate videos or television programmes which demonstrate the positive features of the new setting or situation
- Providing opportunities for imaginative play to let children express their feelings and fears about the transition
- Visiting the children's current setting or going on home visits to meet the children in a familiar setting particularly if working with children with special needs
- Organising introductory visits for the children and their parents/carers so that the children can become familiar with the setting and the adults who will care for and support them
- Providing information appropriate to both children and parents e.g. information pack or brochure plus an activity pack for each child
- Obtaining relevant information from parents about their child e.g. correct name and address, contact details, medical information, dietary requirements, food preferences
- Planning activities for an induction programme (children's first week in new setting).

Transitions from 11 to 16 years and beyond

Children and young people need the opportunity to visit the next setting (e.g. secondary school, sixth form or further education college) more than once so that they can become familiar with the layout. Open evenings to meet their new teachers or tutors are also useful especially if they can meet them on more than one occasion. Being involved in activities at what will be their next school (or college) is also helpful e.g. learning festival, summer school, taster days. (Lindon, 2007)

You can help prepare children and young people aged 11 to 16 years for transitions by:

- Encouraging children and parents to attend open days and evenings at the setting
- Visiting the children's current setting to meet the children in a familiar setting particularly if working with children with special needs
- Arranging taster days for children to experience the layout and routine of the setting e.g. in secondary schools moving to different classrooms for lessons with different subject teachers through fun activities in science, IT and sport
- Discussing individual children's performance with relevant members of staff
- Exchanging relevant documentation e.g. child observations and assessments, SATs test results, any special educational needs information including Individual Education Plans, Behaviour Support Plans, statements, etc.
- Looking at children's records of achievement including their interests and hobbies
- Encouraging children with challenging behaviour to look at this as a fresh start
- Providing the setting's information pack or brochure for children and parents including information on bullying as this is often a key area of concern
- Obtaining relevant information from parents about their child e.g. correct name and address, contact details, medical information, dietary requirements, food preferences
- Providing opportunities for work experience to help children with the transition from the learning environment to the world of work
- Providing opportunities for careers advice and information on further education or training e.g. using the Connexions service for 13 to 19 year olds
- Encouraging children and parents to attend open days/evenings for local colleges.

Key Task

Make a leaflet which includes the following:

- The transitions that are experienced by most children e.g. starting school
- The transitions that are experienced by some children e.g. bereavement
- Examples of how transitions may affect children's behaviour and development
- The role of the adult in supporting transitions.

NOS Links:

Level 2: **STL 2.1** **STL 2.2** **STL 2.3** **STL 2.4** **STL 4.1** **STL 4.2** **STL 4.3** **STL 4.4**

Summary of key points in this chapter:

- **Observing children's development** including: the purpose of observation; the basic principles of child observation; confidentiality; observation methods; recording observations and assessments.
- **Planning provision to promote development** including: the planning cycle; implementing and evaluating plans to promote development.
- **Understanding child and young person development** including: the basic patterns of child and young person development; the sequences of development from 0 to 16 years covering the five different aspects: social, physical, intellectual, communication and emotional.

- **Supporting social development** including: socialisation; behaviour; role models; ways to promote children and young people's social development.
- **Supporting physical development** including: gross motor skills; fine motor skills; coordination; observing and planning to promote physical development; ways to help promote children and young people's physical development.
- **Supporting intellectual development** including: the interrelated components of intellectual development – perception, thinking, language, problem-solving, concepts, memory, concentration and creativity; ways to promote children and young people's intellectual development.
- **Understanding communication and language development** including: effective communication; the modes of language – non-verbal communication, listening, speaking, thinking, reading and writing; ways to promote children and young people's communication and language development.
- **Supporting emotional development** including: personality and temperament; attachments; feelings; self-esteem, self-image and identity; ways to promote children and young people's emotional development.
- **Identifying transitions** including: common transitions; personal transitions; family circumstances.
- **How transitions may affect children's behaviour and development** including: the positive and negative effects of transitions; starting nursery or primary school; moving from primary to secondary school; changing schools.
- **Supporting transitions** including: ten principles to support children's transitions; transitions and children aged 3 to 11 years; transitions from 11 to 16 years and beyond.

Further Reading

Bentham, S. (2003) *A Teaching Assistant's Guide to Child Development and Psychology in the Classroom.* Routledge.

Evangelou, M. (2008) *What Makes a Successful Transition from Primary to Secondary School?* DCSF. http://www.standards.dfes.gov.uk/research/themes/transition/successfultransition/

Fabian, H. and Dunlop, A. (2002) *Transitions in the Early Years.* Routledge Falmer.

Harding, J. and Meldon-Smith, L. (2000) *Helping Young Children to Develop.* Hodder & Stoughton.

Harding, J. and Meldon-Smith, L. (2001) *How to Make Observations and Assessments.* 2nd edition. Hodder Arnold.

Hobart, C. and Frankel, J. (2009) *A Practical Guide to Activities for Young Children.* 4th edition. Nelson Thornes.

Lindon, J. (2007) *Understanding Children and Young People: Development from 5 – 18 Years.* Hodder Arnold.

Meggit, C. (2006) *Child Development: An Illustrated Guide.* 2nd edition. Heinemann Educational Publishers.

Sharman, C, Cross, W and Vennis, D. (2004) *Observing Children: A Practical Guide.* Continuum.

Sheridan, M. *(2007) From Birth to Five Years: Children's Developmental Progress.* 3rd edition. Routledge.

Smidt, S. (2005) Observing, Assessing, Planning. Routledge.

2. Safeguarding the welfare of children and young people

> **This chapter relates to QCF unit:**
> TDA 2.2 Safeguarding the welfare of children and young people

Statutory and regulatory health and safety requirements

You will need to know, understand and follow the legal and organisational requirements of the school for establishing and maintaining the health, safety and security of yourself and others (pupils, staff, families and visitors in the school) at all times as well as the procedures for reporting any concerns or problems to the appropriate person. You will also need to use safe working practices in all that you do which includes ensuring that someone in authority (e.g. the class teacher and/or your line manager) knows where you are at all times in case of an emergency.

Health and safety legislation places overall responsibility for health and safety with the employer. However, as an employee working within a school, you also have responsibilities with regard to maintaining health and safety. All employees have a responsibility under the Health and Safety at Work Act 1974:

- To take reasonable care for the health and safety of themselves and of any person who might be affected by their acts or omissions at work.
- To co-operate with the relevant authorities (e.g. Ofsted) in meeting statutory requirements.
- To not interfere with or misuse anything provided in the interests of health, safety and welfare.
- To make themselves aware of all safety rules, procedures and safe working practices applicable to their posts. (When in doubt they must seek immediate clarification from the delegated person responsible for health and safety in the setting.)
- To ensure that tools and equipment are in good condition and report any defects to the delegated person.
- To use protective clothing and safety equipment provided and to ensure that these are kept in good condition.
- To ensure that any accidents, whether or not an injury occurs, are reported to the delegated person.
- To report potential hazards or any possible deficiencies in health and safety arrangements to the delegated person.

The Workplace (Health, Safety and Welfare) Regulations 1992 clarify and consolidate existing legislation. They also establish a consistent set of standards for the majority of workplaces. The regulations expand on the responsibilities placed on employers (and others in control of premises) by the Health and Safety at Work Act 1974 including: health and safety in the workplace; welfare facilities for people at work and maintenance of the workplace. The workplace and equipment need to be maintained in an efficient state, in working order, and in good repair. Buildings, including mobile or temporary rooms, should be in a good state of repair and services should be in efficient working order. In general, indoor workplaces should be reasonably comfortable, reasonably clean, properly illuminated and adequately spacious.

The environmental requirements of the regulations apply to the workplace, but existing education standards for children's working space, temperature and ventilation and so on, may be more appropriate for education settings. The Education (School Premises) Regulations 1999 provide the statutory requirements for the minimum standards of both new and existing schools. The regulations include a general requirement that all parts of the school's premises must be reasonably maintained to ensure the health, safety and welfare of all users. These regulations also include the specific requirements for: acoustics, ancillary facilities, drainage, heating, lighting, medical accommodation, playing fields, washrooms, staff accommodation, structural matters, ventilation, water supply and weather protection.

The Management of Health and Safety at Work Regulations 1999 require a risk assessment of facilities, a safety policy regarding these risks and appropriate health and safety training. You should be able to recognise any risks within the learning environment and take the appropriate action to minimise them e.g. reporting potential health and safety hazards to the relevant person. (See section on risk assessment in Chapter 6.)

The Manual Handling Operations Regulations 1992, as amended in 2002, apply to manual handling activities such as lifting, lowering, pushing, pulling and carrying. The load being handled may be a box, trolley, person or animal. The Regulations require employers to:

- *Avoid* the need for hazardous manual handling, so far as is reasonably practicable.
- *Assess* the risk of injury from any hazardous manual handling that cannot be avoided.
- *Reduce* the risk of injury from hazardous manual handling, so far as is reasonably practicable.

The regulations require employees to:

- Follow appropriate systems of work laid down for their safety.
- Make proper use of equipment provided for their safety.
- Cooperate with their employer on health and safety matters.
- Inform the employer if they identify hazardous handling activities.
- Take care to ensure their activities do not put others at risk.

(HSE, 2004)

You should be aware of the risks associated with lifting and carrying children, e.g. possible back injuries. Ensure that you follow your school's procedures for lifting and carrying pupils. The Health and Safety Executive (HSE) provides guidance on manual handling (see Further Reading). (See also section on risk assessment in Chapter 6.)

With the continuing development of new and mobile technologies, schools also have a responsibility to help children and young people to stay safe online. E-safety is a safeguarding issue as part of the wider duty of care for all who work in schools. You should have a good understanding of e-safety issues and risks, and how these might relate to the pupils you work with, including data protection and child protection (see section on the school policy for ICT in school in Chapter 10).

 **Activity!**

Find out about the statutory and regulatory requirements that apply to your school including e-safety.

Recognising and dealing with common childhood illnesses

Babies and young children should be vaccinated against diseases including: diphtheria, measles, meningitis, mumps, polio, rubella, tetanus and whooping cough. The first immunisations start when a baby is two months old. The child's parents will usually receive appointments by post to attend their local clinic or GP surgery. You need to be aware of the range of common illnesses that may affect children. These include: allergies, asthma, bronchitis, chicken pox, colds, diabetes, diarrhoea, earache, flu, glandular fever, headache, measles, meningitis, mumps, sore throat and worms.

Recognising signs and symptoms

By knowing the usual behaviour and appearance of the pupils you work with, you will be able to recognise any significant changes that might indicate possible illness. You need to be able to recognise the differences between pupils who are: pretending to be ill; feeling 'under the weather'; and experiencing a health problem. The signs of possible illness in children include:

- Changes in facial colour, e.g. becoming pale or very red.
- Changes in temperature, e.g. becoming very hot or cold, becoming clammy or shivering (a fever usually indicates that the child has an infection).
- Changes in behaviour, e.g. not wanting to play when would usually be very keen.
- Being upset or generally distressed.
- Having reduced concentration levels or even falling asleep.
- Scratching excessively (check the setting's policy regarding head lice).
- Complaining of persistent pain, e.g. headache or stomach-ache.
- Coughing or sneezing excessively.
- Diarrhoea and/or vomiting.
- Displaying a rash. (This could indicate an infection or allergic reaction. Make sure you are aware of any children who may have severe allergic reactions – see section on supporting pupils with special medical needs.)

(Watkinson, 2003)

Responding to signs and symptoms

You should know what to do if pupils come to the setting when they are unwell. The most common childhood illness in children is the common cold. A young child may have as many as 5 to 6 colds a year. Pupils do not need to be kept away from school because of a cold unless their symptoms are very bad. Make sure that a box of tissues is available for pupils to use

ILLNESS	INCUBATION PERIOD	INFECTIOUS PERIOD	HOW TO RECOGNISE IT	WHAT TO DO
	(The time between catching an illness and becoming unwell)	(When your child can give the illness to someone else)		
CHICKENPOX	11–21 days	From the day before the rash appears until all the spots are dry.	Begins with feeling unwell, a rash and maybe a slight temperature. Spots are red and become fluid-filled blisters within a day or so. Appear first on the chest and back, then spread, and eventually dry into scabs, which drop off. Unless spots are badly infected, they don't usually leave a scar.	No need to see your GP unless you're unsure whether it's chickenpox, or your child is very unwell and/or distressed. Give plenty to drink. Paracetamol will help bring down a temperature. Baths, loose, comfortable clothes and calamine lotion can all ease the itchiness. You should also inform the school/nursery in case other children are at risk. Keep your child away from anyone who is, or who is trying to become, pregnant. If your child was with anyone pregnant just before he or she became unwell, let that woman know about the chickenpox (and tell her to see her GP). Sometimes chickenpox in pregnancy can cause miscarriage or the baby may be born with chickenpox.
MEASLES	7–12 days	From a few days before until 4 days after the appearance of the rash.	Begins like a bad cold and cough with sore, watery eyes. Child becomes gradually more unwell, with a temperature. Rash appears after third or fourth day. Spots are red and slightly raised; may be blotchy, but are not itchy. Begins behind the ears, and spreads to the face and neck and then the rest of the body. Children can become very unwell, with cough and high temperature. The illness usually lasts about a week.	See your GP. If your child is unwell give him or her rest and plenty to drink. Warm drinks will ease the cough. Paracetamol will ease discomfort and lower the temperature. Vaseline around the lips protects the skin. Wash crustiness from eyelids with warm water.
MUMPS	14–21 days	From a few days before becoming unwell until swelling goes down. Maybe 10 days in all.	At first, your child may be mildly unwell with a bit of fever, and may complain of pain around the ear or feel uncomfortable when chewing. Swelling then starts under the jaw up to the ear. Swelling often starts on one side, followed (though not always) by the other. Your child's face is back to normal size in about a week, it's rare for mumps to affect boys' testes (balls). This happens rather more often in adult men with mumps. For both boys and men, the risk of any permanent damage to the testes is very low.	Your child may not feel especially ill and may not want to be is bed. Baby or junior paracetamol will ease pain is the swollen glands. Check correct dosage on pack. Give plenty to drink, but not fruit juice. This makes the saliva flow, which can hurt. No need to see your GP unless your child has stomach ache and is being sick, or develops a rash of small red/purple spots or bruises.
PARVOVIRUS B19 (ALSO CALLED FIFTH DISEASE OR SLAPPED CHEEK DISEASE)	Variable 1–20 days	It is most infections in the days before the rash appears.	Begins with a fever and nasal discharge. A bright red rash similar to a slap appears on the cheeks. Over the next 2–4 days, a lacy type of rash spreads to the trunk and limbs.	Although this is most common in children, it can occur in adults. In the majority of cases it has no serious consequences, but it may cause complications for people with chronic anaemic conditions (e.g. sickle cell disease). Rarely, in pregnant women who are not immune to the disease, the intention may result in stillbirth or affect the baby in the womb. Pregnant women who come into contact with the infection or develop a rash should see their GP as soon as possible.
RUBELLA (GERMAN MEASLES)	14–21 days	One week before and at least 4 days after the rash first appears.	Can be difficult to diagnose with certainty. Starts like a mild cold. The rash appears in a day or two, first on the face, then spreading. Spots are flat. On a light skin, they are pale pink. Glands in the back of the neck may be swollen. Your child won't usually feel unwell.	Give plenty to drink. Keep your child away from anybody you know who's up to 4 months pregnant (or trying to get pregnant). If your child was with anyone pregnant before you knew about the illness, let her know. If an unimmunised pregnant woman catches German measles in the first 4 months of pregnancy, there is a risk of damage to her baby. Any pregnant woman who has had contact with German measles should see her GP. The GP can check whether or not she is immune and, if not, whether there is any sign of her developing the illness.
WHOOPING COUGH	7–14 days	From the first signs of the illness until about 6 weeks after coughing starts. If an antibiotic is given, the infectious period is up to 5 days after beginning the course of treatment	Begins like a cold and cough. The cough gradually gets worse. After about 2 weeks, coughing bouts start. These are exhausting and make it difficult to breathe. Your child may choke and vomit. Sometimes, but not always, there's a whooping noise as the child draws in breath after coughing. It takes some weeks before the coughing fits start to die down.	It your child has a cough that gets worse rather than better and starts to have longer fits of coughing more and more often, see your doctor. It's important for the sake of other children to know whether or not it's whooping cough. Talk to your GP about how best to look after your child and avoid contact with babies, who are most at risk from serious complications.

Figure 2.1: *Childhood illnessess from DH, 2006; p.101*

and that used tissues are disposed of properly to avoid the spread of germs. Colds and flu are caused by viruses and so cannot be helped by antibiotics. However, cold and flu viruses can weaken the body and lead to a secondary bacterial infection such as tonsillitis, otitis media (middle ear infection), sinusitis, bronchitis and pneumonia. These bacterial infections require antibiotic treatment. You also need to know what to do if a pupil becomes ill while at the setting. You should seek medical advice if you have concerns about any of the following:

- The child's high temperature lasts for more than 24 hours.
- The child has a persistent cough with green or yellow catarrh (possible bronchitis or pneumonia).
- The child has pain above the eyes or in the face (possible sinusitis).
- The child has a severe sore throat (possible tonsillitis).
- The child has a bad earache (possible ear infection).

Seek medical advice *immediately* if:

- you think the child may have meningitis
- the child has breathing difficulties
- the child's asthma deteriorates
- the child has a convulsion
- the child has very poor fluid intake or cannot swallow liquids
- a baby persistently refuses to take feeds
- the child has been to a country where there is a risk of malaria in the last 12 months.

Recording and reporting signs of illness

Ensure that you know what to do when pupils are sick, for example, where or to whom to send sick pupils. You may need to stay with a sick pupil while someone else summons assistance. If you have any concerns regarding the health of the pupils you work with, you should always inform the class teacher. You need to be able to recognise any changes to a pupil's behaviour or appearance that may indicate a possible health problem and report these appropriately. Whatever the illness, you should know where and when to seek assistance. You should also know what types of written records are required and to whom you should report any concerns regarding any pupil's health. Check whether you are allowed to contact parents/carers directly regarding a sick pupil or whether this is the responsibility of someone else, e.g. the class teacher or head teacher.

In Practice

Thom is returning from the school office when he sees a pupil being sick in a corridor. What should he do?

Following the procedures for storing and administering medicines

Parents are responsible for their own children's medication. Children under the age of 16 should not be given medication without their parent's written consent. The head teacher usually decides whether the school can assist a pupil who needs medication during the school day. The school will have a form for the parent to sign if their child requires medication while at school. Many pupils with long-term medical needs will not require medication while at the school. If they do, pupils can usually administer it themselves depending on their age, level of development, medical needs and type of medication. The school's policy should encourage self-administration where appropriate and provide suitable facilities for pupils to do so in safety and privacy. (See section below on supporting pupils with long-term medical needs.)

Teaching assistants have no legal duty to administer medication or to supervise a pupil taking it. This is a voluntary role similar to that of being a designated first aider (see above). The head teacher, parents and relevant health professionals should support teaching assistants who volunteer to administer medication by providing information, training and reassurance about their legal liability. Arrangements should be made for when the teaching assistant responsible for providing assistance is absent or not available.

The health and safety of pupils and staff must be considered at all times. Safety procedures must be in place regarding the safe storage, handling and disposal of medicines. Some medication (e.g. reliever inhaler for asthma or adrenalin device for severe anaphylaxis) must be quickly available in an emergency and should not be locked away. The relevant staff members and the pupils concerned must know where this medication is stored.

You also need to know the location of safety equipment in the different areas of the learning environment. You must be clear about the safety arrangements for the areas and pupils you work with including: the position of fire exits, extinguishers, blanket, first aid boxes; your role during fire drill and what to do in case of fire or other emergency especially the procedures for pupils with physical disabilities or sensory impairments, escape routes and alternatives if blocked by fire, etc. (Information about responding to emergency situations such as following evacuation procedures and dealing with accidents is in Chapter 6.)

 **Activity!**

- Where is the safety equipment located in your setting?
- Where are the first aid boxes located?

 Key Task

1. Find out about your school's procedures for: dealing with common childhood illnesses; and storing and administering medicines.
2. Describe your role and responsibilities in the event of an illness.

NOS Links:

Level 2:   STL 3.2

Safeguarding children and young people from abuse

All schools should establish and maintain a safe environment for pupils and deal with circumstances where there are child welfare concerns. Through their child protection policies and procedures for safeguarding children, schools have an important role in the detection and prevention of child abuse and neglect. This also includes helping children and young people to protect themselves from abuse and dealing with bullying.

What is child abuse?

The Children Act 1989 defines child abuse as a person's actions that cause a child to suffer *significant harm* to their health, development or well-being. Significant harm can be caused by: punishing a child too much; hitting or shaking a child; constantly criticising, threatening or rejecting a child; sexually interfering with or assaulting a child; neglecting a child, e.g. not giving them enough to eat or not ensuring their safety. The Department of Health (DH) defines child abuse as the abuse or neglect of a child by inflicting harm or by failing to prevent harm. Children may be abused by someone known to them, e.g. parent, sibling, babysitter, carer or other familiar adult. It is very rare for a child to be abused by a stranger (DfES, 2006).

 key words

Child abuse: a person's actions that cause a child to suffer significant harm to their health, development or well-being.

Types of child abuse

- **Physical abuse** involves causing deliberate physical harm to a child and may include: burning, drowning, hitting, poisoning, scalding, shaking, suffocating or throwing. Physical abuse also includes deliberately causing, or fabricating the symptoms of, ill health in a child (e.g. Munchausen's Syndrome by Proxy).
- **Emotional abuse** involves the persistent psychological mistreatment of a child and may include: making the child feel inadequate, unloved or worthless; imposing inappropriate developmental expectations on the child; threatening, taunting or humiliating the child; exploiting or corrupting the child.
- **Sexual abuse** involves coercing or encouraging a child to engage in sexual activities to which the child does not or cannot consent because of their age or level of understanding. These sexual activities may involve physical contact such as penetrative and/or oral sex or encouraging the child to watch the adult masturbate or to look at pornographic material.
- **Neglect** involves the persistent failure to meet a child's essential basic needs for food, clothing, shelter, loving care or medical attention. Neglect may also include when a child is put at risk by being left alone without proper adult supervision.

(DfES, 2006)

Identifying signs of possible abuse

As a teaching assistant, you need to be aware of the signs and indicators of possible child abuse and neglect and to whom you should report any concerns or suspicions. You may have contact with pupils on a daily basis and so have an essential role to play in recognising indications of possible abuse or neglect such as outward signs of physical abuse, uncharacteristic behaviour patterns or failure to develop in the expected ways.

Indications of possible physical abuse include:

- recurrent unexplained injuries or burns
- refusal to discuss injuries
- improbable explanations for injuries
- watchful, cautious attitude towards adults

 key words

Emotional abuse: the persistent psychological mistreatment of a child such as making the child feel inadequate, unloved or worthless; threatening, taunting or humiliating the child.

Neglect: the persistent failure to meet a child's essential basic needs for food, clothing, shelter, loving care or medical attention.

Physical abuse: actions which cause deliberate physical harm to a child such as burning, drowning, hitting, poisoning, scalding, shaking, suffocating or throwing.

Sexual abuse: actions which coerce or encourage a child to engage in sexual activities to which the child does not or cannot consent because of their age or level of understanding.

- reluctance to play and be spontaneous
- shrinking from physical contact
- avoidance of activities involving removal of clothes, e.g. swimming
- aggressive or bullying behaviour
- being bullied
- lack of concentration
- difficulty in trusting people and making friends.

Indications of possible emotional abuse include:

- delayed speech development
- very passive and lacking in spontaneity
- social isolation, e.g. finding it hard to play with other children
- unable to engage in imaginative play
- low self-esteem
- easily distracted
- fear of new situations
- self-damaging behaviour, e.g. head-banging, pulling out hair
- self-absorbing behaviour, e.g. obsessive rocking, thumb-sucking
- eating problems, e.g. overeating or lack of appetite
- withdrawn behaviour and depression.

Indications of possible sexual abuse include:

- sudden behaviour changes when abuse begins
- low self-esteem
- using sexual words in play activities uncharacteristic for age/level of development
- withdrawn or secretive behaviour
- starting to wet or soil themselves
- demonstrating inappropriate seductive or flirtatious behaviour
- frequent public masturbation
- frightened of physical contact
- depression resulting in self-harm (or an overdose)
- bruises, scratches, burns or bite marks on the body.

Indications of possible neglect include:

- slow physical development
- constant hunger and/or tiredness
- poor personal hygiene and appearance
- frequent lateness or absenteeism
- undiagnosed/untreated medical conditions
- social isolation, e.g. poor social skills
- compulsive stealing or begging.

(Indications of possible bullying are dealt with below.)

- You may be asked to carry out a specific type of assessment, or provide help or a specific service to the child as part of an agreed plan and contribute to the reviewing of the child's progress (including attending child protection conferences).

(DfES, 2006)

Teaching assistants working closely with pupils in schools are well placed to identify the early signs of abuse, neglect or bullying. In addition, many pupils may view the school as neutral territory where they may feel more able to talk with an adult they trust about what is happening to them. If you have concerns that a pupil in your school may be experiencing possible abuse or neglect than you *must* report these concerns promptly to the relevant person, e.g. class teacher, head teacher or teacher responsible for child protection issues.

Flow chart 1: Referral

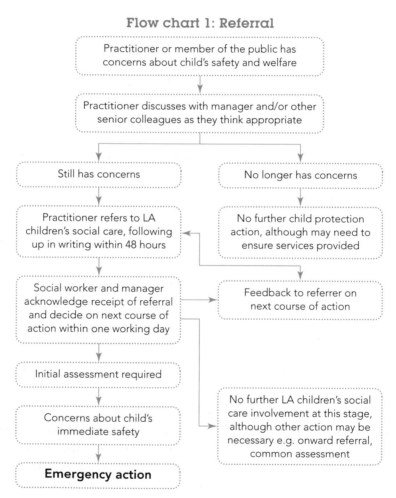

Figure 2.2: *Flow chart: Referral process for safeguarding children from Working Together to Safeguard Children, 2010; p.186.*

In Practice

Lee is working as a teaching assistant with pupils aged 7 to 8 years. Lee has concerns about a particular pupil's welfare after noticing multiple bruises on the child's arms. What would you do if you had concerns about a pupil's welfare? Who would you report your concerns to? How would you report your concerns?

Responding to a child's disclosure of abuse

A child may make a personal disclosure to a member of staff relating to an experience in which the child may have been significantly harmed. A child may make a disclosure to you at an inappropriate place or time. If this happens, you should talk again individually to the child before the end of the day. You may be able to discuss the issue with a senior colleague without giving the name of the child. If not, you should follow the setting's confidentiality policy and child protection procedures.

If a child makes a personal disclosure that s/he has been abused in some way, you should:

- Listen to what the child has to say.
- Accept what the child is saying.
- Allow the child to talk openly.
- Listen to the child rather than ask direct questions.
- Not criticise the alleged perpetrator of the abuse.
- Reassure the child that what has happened is not his or her fault.
- Stress to the child that it was the right thing to tell someone.
- Reassure the child but not make promises that you might not be able to keep.
- Not promise the child to keep the disclosed information confidential (as it might be necessary for the matter to be referred to social services).
- Explain simply to the child what has to be done next and who has to be told.

After a child has made a disclosure to you:

1. Make brief notes as soon as possible after the conversation.
2. Do not destroy the original notes, as the courts may need these.
3. Record the date, time, place and any noticeable non-verbal behaviour as well as the words used by the child.
4. Draw a diagram to indicate the position of any bruising or other injury.
5. Only record statements and observations rather than interpretations or assumptions.

Dealing with a disclosure from a child or being involved in a child protection case can be a very distressing and stressful experience. You may require support for yourself and should discuss with a senior colleague how to access support when dealing with a case of child abuse or neglect.

Allegations of abuse against staff or volunteers

If a pupil, or parent, makes a complaint of abuse against a member of staff or volunteer, the person receiving the complaint must take it seriously and follow the relevant procedures in line with LSCB procedures. Professionals who are independent of the school should investigate all allegations of abuse against staff or volunteers.

If you have reason to suspect that a pupil may have been abused by another member of staff, either in the school or elsewhere, you must immediately inform a senior colleague. You should make a record of the concerns including a note of anyone else who witnessed the incident or allegation. The head teacher will not investigate the incident themselves but will assess whether it is necessary to refer the matter to social services.

If the head teacher decides that the allegation warrants further action through child protection procedures a referral will be made direct to social services. If the allegation constitutes a serious criminal offence it will be necessary to contact social services and the learning to trust their inner feelings, they can avoid many potentially risky situations. Use role-play to help them think about what they should do if their friends want them to do something they dislike or feel uncomfortable about, e.g. going to a party, getting drunk, having sex, shoplifting, taking drugs, etc. Peer pressure can be very strong; encourage them to decide and set limits about what they will and will not do so that they know how to cope before the situation arises. Make sure that pupils understand the dangers of situations that may put their personal safety at risk such as: being left at home alone; playing in deserted or dark places; being out on their own; getting lost, e.g. on outings; walking home alone especially in the dark; talking to strangers; accepting lifts from strangers including hitchhiking.

As pupils get older they need opportunities to explore their environment and to develop their independence. To do this safely they will need to know and understand about acceptable risk taking. Risk taking can be explored through stories (e.g. *Jack and the Beanstalk*) and television programmes. Pupils can think about and discuss the risks taken by their favourite characters. Encourage them to identify some of the risks they take in their own lives and look at ways they can minimise risk. Puppets and role-play can be used to help them deal with potentially risky situations. Ensure the pupils know and understand The Keepsafe Code (see **www. kidscape.org.uk**).

 **Activity!**

Think about ways of encouraging children to be aware of their own bodies and understand their rights not to be abused, e.g. activities involving discussion about their own bodies, activities to encourage children to help protect themselves, activities to tackle bullying.

Helping pupils to access appropriate support when necessary

Pupils need to know where to go for help and support in difficult situations. They should be encouraged to identify people in the school and the local community who can help them to keep safe, e.g. worries about bullying or problems at home may be discussed with a member of school staff; if they get lost they can ask a police officer for assistance. Encourage pupils to think of a trusted adult (e.g. parents, other relative, best friend, teacher, teaching assistant) they could talk to about a difficult situation, e.g. abuse, bullying, negative peer pressure, etc. Ensure that they understand that if they go to an adult for help, especially within the school, they will be believed and supported. Provide them with information about other sources of help and support, e.g. Childline, The Samaritans, etc.

 **Activity!**

Find out what support is available in your school and local community for children and young people.

Dealing with bullying

Research suggests that 85 per cent of children aged 5 to 11 years have experienced bullying in some form, e.g. name-calling, being hit or kicked. In 2000 a survey of 11 to 16 year olds, found that '36% of children said they had been bullied in the last 12 months; 26% had been threatened with violence and 13% had been physically attacked' (ATL, 2000). Bullying is such a serious problem that schools must have an anti-bullying policy that clearly sets out the ways in which they try to prevent bullying and deal with bullying behaviour when it happens.

Defining bullying behaviour

Bullying can be defined as behaviour that is deliberately hurtful or aggressive, repeated over a period of time and difficult for victims to defend themselves against. There are three main types of bullying: physical: hitting, kicking, taking belongings; verbal: name-calling, insulting, making offensive remarks; indirect: spreading nasty stories about someone, exclusion from social groups, being made the subject of malicious rumours, sending malicious emails or text messages on mobile phones.

key words

Bullying: behaviour that is deliberately hurtful or aggressive which includes hitting, name-calling or exclusion from social groups.

Name-calling is the most common type of bullying. Pupils may be called nasty names because of their individual characteristics, ethnic origin, nationality, skin colour, sexual orientation or disability. Verbal bullying is common amongst both boys and girls. Boys experience more physical violence and threats when being bullied than girls. However, physical attacks on girls by other girls are becoming more common. Girls tend to use more indirect types of bullying which can be more difficult to detect and deal with (DfES, 2000).

Any pupil can experience bullying but certain factors may make bullying more likely. While there is *never* an acceptable excuse for bullying behaviour, pupils are more likely to experience bullying if they: are shy or have an over-protective family environment; are from a different racial or ethnic group to the majority of pupils; appear different in some obvious respect, e.g. stammering; have special needs, e.g. a disability or learning difficulties; behave inappropriately, e.g. are a 'nuisance' or intrude on others' activities or possess expensive accessories, e.g. mobile phones or computer games.

Recognising when a pupil is being bullied

Pupils who are experiencing bullying may be reluctant to attend school and are often absent. They may be more anxious and insecure than others, have fewer friends and often feel unhappy and lonely. They can suffer from low self-esteem and negative self-image; they may see themselves as failures, e.g. stupid, ashamed and unattractive.

Possible signs that a pupil is being bullied include:

- suddenly not wanting to go to school when usually enjoys it
- unexplained cuts and bruises
- possessions have unexplained damage or are persistently 'lost'
- becoming withdrawn or depressed but will not say what is the matter.

While the above signs may indicate that a pupil is being bullied, they may also be symptomatic of other problems such as abuse (see the section above about responding to concerns about possible abuse).

Helping pupils who are being bullied

The behaviour of some pupils can lead to them experiencing bullying, though this does not justify the behaviour of the bullies. For example, some pupils may: find it difficult to play with other pupils; be hyperactive; behave in ways that irritate others; bully weaker pupils; be easily

3. Maintaining and supporting professional relationships

This chapter relates to QCF units:

TDA 2.3 Communication and professional relationships
with children, young people and adults

TDA 2.7 Maintain and support relationships with children
and young people

Developing positive working relationships with pupils

Being a teaching assistant involves working closely with individuals and groups of children and/or young people. Your relationships with pupils must be professional without being too distant. When working with groups of children you should give individual attention to each child and ensure that *all* the children feel welcome and valued within the school. This includes encouraging pupils to answer questions, ask questions, make suggestions and contribute ideas as appropriate to their ages, needs and abilities.

In order to develop positive working relationships with the pupils you need to know and understand the principles and values that underpin all work with children and young people (see page vi). This will enable you to work with others to:

- ensure that the welfare and well-being of pupils are at the centre of the school
- empower pupils through play and learning
- provide a stimulating and challenging learning environment
- ensure physical and personal safety within the learning environment
- respect every pupil as an individual
- demonstrate a considerate and caring attitude towards pupils
- provide a learning environment which is accessible to all pupils
- provide play and learning activities to extend pupils' understanding of themselves, other people and the world around them
- encourage cooperation between pupils, parents and colleagues.

Positive interactions with pupils

As a teaching assistant you should know and understand what is meant by the terms 'appropriate' and 'inappropriate' behaviour when interacting with pupils, including the relevant legal requirements (see section on rewards and sanctions in Chapter 8). To work well as a teaching assistant you need to genuinely care about children. In addition to meeting children's physical and intellectual needs you also need to provide emotional security by showing a genuine interest in everything the children say and do as well as providing comfort when children are upset or unwell. Children can sense when they are with someone who really cares about them. Personal friendships with children or their parents are best avoided as they can complicate your professional relationships within the school. However, if you are working in your local community this may not always be possible. If you *are* friends with children and/or their families outside the school try to keep your personal and professional life separate. For example, do not give the child preferential treatment within the school or gossip with parents about what occurs in the school. (See section below on confidentiality matters.)

 key words

Stereotype: simplistic characterisation or expectation of a person based on perceived differences or prejudices relating to their race, culture, gender, disability or age.

Ten ways to develop positive relationships with pupils

You can develop positive relationships with pupils by:

1. Remembering children's names and pronouncing them correctly.
2. Being approachable and willing to listen to pupils.
3. Listening and responding to pupils in ways which let children feel they are understood.
4. Giving time to pupils as individuals within the school.
5. Avoiding **stereotype** judgements about individual pupils concerning race, gender, ability or religion.
6. Getting a pupil's own explanation concerning behaviour before criticising them; do not jump to conclusions.
7. Communicating with pupils in a sensitive way, e.g. do not interrupt them rudely or talk over them (see section below on effective communication with pupils).
8. Showing pupils that they are valued and important people.
9. Being alert to children's feelings.
10. Looking at the world from a child's point of view!

 Key Task

Outline how you contribute to developing and promoting positive relationships with pupils in your school.

NOS Links:

Level 2:   STL 4.1

Communicating with children and young people

It is important to communicate with children in a manner that is clear and concise and appropriate to their ages, needs and abilities. This involves: using words and phrases that children will understand; actively listening to children; responding positively to children's views and feelings and clarifying and confirming points to reinforce children's knowledge and understanding. When communicating with children: ask and answer questions to prompt appropriate responses from them and to check their understanding; encourage them to ask questions and contribute their own ideas and adapt communication methods to suit their individual language needs if they have special needs, such as a hearing impairment or if they are bilingual. (For more information on supporting bilingual pupils see Chapter 11.)

Effective communication with children

The first step towards effective communication with children (and adults, too, of course) is being able to listen attentively to what they have to say. Nearly all breakdowns in communication are due to people not listening to each other. Effective communication requires good inter-personal skills such as:

- Availability – make time to listen to pupils.
- Attentive listening – concentrate on what pupils are saying.
- Appropriate use of non-verbal skills – facing the pupil, leaning slightly towards them, smiling, nodding, open-handed gestures not clenched fists.
- Follow the rules of turn-taking in language exchanges; every person needs to have their say while others listen.
- Politeness and courtesy – no shouting, no talking over other people, avoiding sarcasm (especially with younger pupils, who do not understand it and can be frightened by your strange tone of voice).
- Being relaxed, confident and articulate.
- Using appropriate vocabulary for your listener(s).
- Encouraging others to talk by asking 'open' questions.
- Responding positively to what is said.
- Being receptive to new ideas.
- Being sympathetic to other viewpoints (even if you totally disagree with them!).
- Providing opportunities for meaningful communication to take place.

Effective communication also involves pupils being able to understand and use the language of learning. That is, the language needed to: understand concepts; participate in problem-solving and develop ideas and opinions. You need to be able to utilise language effectively yourself in order to encourage and extend pupils' learning. A sound knowledge of child development (see Chapter 1) plus the realistic organisation of the school, classroom, activities and time are essential components for effective communication with pupils.

Active listening

Communication is a two-way process that depends on the sender (talker) and on the receiver (listener). Research has shown that adults tend to be poor listeners. Adults working in schools do too much talking and not enough listening to pupils' talk. While most primary schools appreciate the benefit of 'listening time', many secondary schools do not (Hutchcroft, 1981). Active listening depends on: listening carefully to pupils' talk; considering the mood of the participants; minimising distractions in the immediate surroundings.

Figure 3.1: Adult communicating with children

Asking and answering questions

You need to develop your skills of being able to initiate and sustain pupils' talk by providing questions, prompts and cues, which encourage and support the pupils' language and learning without doing the thinking for them. Some questions require only limited responses or answers from pupils. These 'closed' questions usually receive one-word answers such as 'yes' or 'no' or the name of a person/object. These types of questions do not help pupils to develop their own language and communication skills. 'Open' questions, on the other hand, are a positive way to encourage a variety of responses allowing more detailed answers, descriptions and accounts of pupils' personal experiences, feelings and ideas. For example: the question 'Did you ride your bike?' can only be answered by 'yes' or 'no'. Instead you could ask 'Where did you go on your bike?' and then use questions like 'What happened next?' to prompt further responses.

As well as asking questions, you need to be able to *answer* pupils' questions. Encouraging pupils to ask questions helps them to explore their environment more fully, to look for reasons/possible answers and to reach their own conclusions as to why and how things happen. Always treat their questions seriously. Try to answer them truthfully and accurately. If you honestly do not know the answer, then say so and suggest an alternative way for the pupil to obtain an answer. For example, 'I don't know where that animal comes from, let's look in the encyclopaedia or on the Internet to find out'. Or 'I'm not sure what that word means exactly; go and look in your dictionary to see if it's in there'. You should encourage pupils to find their own answers as appropriate to their age and level of development. Give them information in an appropriate form, which will increase their vocabulary and add to their knowledge/understanding of their world. Your answers should use words that are appropriate to the pupil. For example, if a younger pupil asks: 'Why does it rain?' you need to give a simple reply such as 'Clouds are full of water which falls back to the ground as drops of rain' while an older pupil can be given a more technical description of cloud formation and rainfall.

Key Task

Listen to adults talking with children in a variety of situations, both within and outside your school (e.g. on buses, in shops, in the street, in the playground). Pay particular attention to the questions asked by the adults and the children, and how they are answered. Consider these points:

- Which inter-personal skills were used?
- How effective was the communication?
- Did the adult use active listening skills?
- What did the children learn about language, the activity and/or the environment?

NOS Links:

Level 2:   STL 2.3   STL 4.1   STL 4.3

The importance of praise and encouragement

Praise and encouragement are essential components when communicating with children. All children (especially young children) need immediate and positive affirmations or rewards to show that their learning and development are progressing in accordance with the adult's (and child's) expectations. Adults should emphasise the positive aspects of children's learning and development. You can support children in managing failure and disappointment by emphasising the importance of taking part, trying their personal best and praising and/or rewarding children for their *efforts* not just their achievements. Children gain confidence and increased positive self-esteem when they receive praise/rewards for their efforts and achievements including encouragement to try new activities and experiences.

There are four main methods used to praise and encourage pupils:

1. **Verbal**: e.g. 'praise' assemblies; positive comments about the child's behaviour or activities such as 'Well done, Tom! This is a lovely story! Tell me what happened next'.
2. **Non-verbal**: e.g. body language: leaning forward or turning towards a child to show interest in what the child is communicating; facial expressions: smiling; sign language: 'good boy/girl!'.
3. **Symbolic**: e.g. 'smiley faces' for a carefully done work or positive behaviour; stickers for being a good listener or for reading well; stars or merit points for attempting and/or completing tasks.
4. **Written**: e.g. merit certificates; written comments in head teacher's book; newsletter recording achievements; comments written (or stamped) on child's work such as 'Well done!' or 'Good work!'.

Activity!

What methods do you use to provide positive praise and encouragement for the efforts and achievements of pupils in your school?

Supporting pupils in developing relationships

As a teaching assistant you will support children in developing positive relationships with other children and adults. Observe how the behaviour of parents and other significant adults (teachers, teaching assistants, play workers and so on) affects children's behaviour, how children deal with their own and other people's feelings and how children relate to others.

This is why it is so important for adults to provide positive role models for children's behaviour. Positive interactions with adults (and other children) in various settings encourages children to demonstrate positive ways of relating to others and using appropriate social skills. To develop positive relationships every child needs:

- **Security**
- **Praise**
- **Encouragement**
- **Communication**
- **Interaction**
- **Acceptance**
- **Love**.

You should set limits and firm boundaries as agreed with children, families, colleagues and other professionals. To do this you will need to effectively communicate and exchange information with children according to their ages, needs and abilities. This includes understanding the possible effects of communication difficulties and attention deficit disorders. You will also need to be able to implement agreed behaviour procedures and strategies when dealing with children who continue to demonstrate challenging behaviour.

Supporting pupils in developing agreements about behaviour

Adults should not use aggressive or bullying tactics when trying to encourage appropriate behaviour in children. Firm discipline includes warmth and affection to show children they are cared for and accepted for who they are regardless of any inappropriate behaviour they may demonstrate. The school should provide an appropriate framework for socially acceptable behaviour with rules that have to be followed by all. Language plays an important part in encouraging children to behave in acceptable ways as it enables them to: understand verbal explanations of what is and is not acceptable behaviour; understand verbal explanations of why certain behaviour is not acceptable; express their own needs and feelings more clearly; avoid conflicts when handled by sensitive adults; reach compromises more easily and have a positive outlet for feelings through discussion and imaginative play.

As part of your role as a teaching assistant you will be helping to promote the school's policy, procedures and strategies regarding children's behaviour by consistently and effectively implementing agreements about ways to behave, e.g. ground rules and/or a children's code of conduct (see section on supporting behaviour management strategies in Chapter 8). You will support children in developing agreements about ways of behaving appropriate to the requirements of the school *and* the children's ages and levels of development.

Bury College
Woodbury LRC

Agreements about ways of behaving should be introduced following consultation with colleagues, children and parents. A copy of the <u>home–school agreement</u> should be sent home and parents (and if appropriate, children) asked to sign as an indication of agreement and support. The agreement should be displayed throughout the school as appropriate. The agreement should be brief and easy to learn. It should include rules that the school will enforce. The reason for each rule should be obvious, but staff should also explain these as appropriate to the age and level of development of the children they work with. The agreement may be applied to a variety of situations and should be designed to encourage children to develop responsibility for their own behaviour. Developing agreements about ways of behaving should include negotiating appropriate goals and boundaries for behaviour. (See section on setting goals and boundaries in Chapter 8.)

key words

Home–school agreement: a document setting out the responsibilities of the school, parents and pupils which will encourage positive behaviour to support children's development and learning.

Encouraging pupils to recognise and deal with feelings

An essential aspect of supporting children in developing relationships is helping children to recognise and deal with their own feelings and those of other people. Feelings can be defined as: an *awareness* of pleasure or pain; physical and/or psychological *impressions; experience of personal emotions* such as anger, joy, fear or sorrow, and *interpersonal emotions* such as affection, kindness, malice or jealousy.

In British society we are often encouraged to keep our feelings to ourselves. Males may be discouraged from showing the more sensitive emotions; females may be discouraged from demonstrating the more aggressive emotions. Babies and very young children naturally demonstrate clearly how they feel by crying, shouting and rejecting objects. They will openly show affection and other emotions such as jealousy or anger. Young children do not understand that others can be physically or emotionally hurt by what they say or do. Gradually, children become conditioned to accept that the feelings and needs of others *do* matter.

We need to ensure that children do not forget their own feelings and emotional needs by becoming too concerned with the feelings of others or trying to please others. Children need to know that it is natural to feel a wide range of emotions and that it is acceptable to express strong feelings such as love and anger openly as long as they do so in positive and appropriate ways.

As a teaching assistant you can help pupils to recognise and express their feelings through:

- **Books, stories and poems** about feelings and common events experienced by other children/young people to help them recognise and deal with these in their own lives.
- **Creative activities** to provide positive outlets for feelings, e.g. pummelling clay to express anger; painting/drawing pictures or writing stories and poems which reflect their feelings about particular events and experiences.
- **Physical play or sports** involving vigorous physical activity that allow a positive outlet for anger or frustration.
- **Drama or role-play** activities to act out feelings, e.g. jealousy concerning siblings; worries over past experiences; fears about future events such as visit to dentist.

home school agreement

school

The school will:

○ Ensure your child's physical and social well being at all times, and to foster feelings of confidence, self-worth and belonging.

○ Deliver a balanced and carefully planned curriculum which meets the needs of your individual child.

○ Provide a range of after school extra-curricular activities designed to enrich your child's experience.

○ Ensure that all homework tasks are given regularly on an agreed day, and that they reflect your child's learning needs.

○ To actively welcome parents/carers into the life of the school and to ensure that teaching staff are always available, by mutual arrangement, to discuss any concerns you might have about your child's progress or general welfare.

○ Keep you informed about the school's policies and guidelines on behaviour and equal opportunities, other general school matters and about your child's progress in particular

○ Ensure that all teaching staff keep up to date on important educational developments and initiatives which might effect your child, and to inform you of these at given meetings where appropriate.

parents/carers

I/We undertake to:

○ Ensure that my child attends school regularly and that absences are properly notified.

○ Ensure that my child arrives and where appropriate is collected promptly at the beginning and end of the school day.

○ Support the school's policies and guidelines on behaviour and equal opportunities.

○ Support my child in his/her homework and wherever possible promote opportunities for home learning.

○ Ensure that my child goes to bed at a reasonable time on weekdays.

○ Attend Parent's Evenings and discussions about my child's progress at school.

pupils

I agree to:

○ Always try to do my best in my lessons.

○ Always try to remember to be polite and thoughtful towards others.

○ Always try to enjoy school and help other children do the same.

agreement

School _____

Parents/Carers _____

Pupil _____

Date _____

Figure 3.2: Example of home–school agreement

Babies and very young children are naturally egocentric; their belief that the world revolves around them and their wishes often makes them appear selfish and possessive. As children develop they begin to think and care about others as well as themselves. We have all experienced jealousy in our relationships with others, e.g. with siblings, friends, neighbours, colleagues, employers. Unchecked jealousy can be a very destructive and hurtful emotion that prevents children (and adults) from developing respect and care for others.

You can help pupils to cope with any feelings of jealousy they may have towards others by:

- **Avoiding comparisons between pupils (especially siblings).** For example, do not make comments like 'You're not as quiet as your brother' or 'Why can't you behave more like that group of children?'.
- **Encouraging pupils to focus on their own abilities.** Emphasise cooperation and sharing rather than competition. Comparisons should be related to improving their own individual skills.
- **Understanding the reasons for a pupil's jealousy.** Children feel better when adults acknowledge their feelings. Do not make children feel guilty about being jealous.
- **Treating all pupils with respect and fairness.** Take each pupil's individual needs into account. Pupils may require different amounts of adult attention at different times. Equality of opportunity does not mean treating everyone exactly the same, as this would mean ignoring individual needs; it means treating individuals fairly and providing the same *chances*.
- **Reassuring pupils that they are accepted for *who* they are regardless of what they do.** Try to spend a few minutes with each pupil in your group. Give regular individual attention to help reduce jealousy and increase emotional security.

 **Activity!**

Describe an activity which supports pupils in understanding other people's feelings, e.g. sharing a story or poem about feelings and common events experienced by other children. Give an example from your own experiences of working with pupils.

Dealing with pupils' emotional outbursts

You should work with the teacher to provide a calm and accepting environment which allows pupils to experience and express their feelings safely (see above section on encouraging pupils to recognise and deal with feelings). Sometimes pupils (especially young children) are overwhelmed by their emotions and will act inappropriately or regress to previous patterns of behaviour. When children are unable to use language to express their feelings (e.g. because they lack the appropriate words, are too worked up, have behavioural/emotional difficulties or other special needs) they are more prone to demonstrate their emotional responses in physical ways e.g. biting, scratching, kicking, shouting, screaming, throwing things, throwing themselves on the floor, etc. An emotional outburst or 'temper tantrum' can be very frightening to the child and others in the group or class. Adults too can find children's emotional outbursts difficult to deal with.

 key words

Emotional outburst: uncontrolled expression of intense emotion, e.g. rage or frustration.

When dealing with a pupil's emotional outbursts it is essential that you:

- Remain calm yourself; speak quietly but confidently, shouting only make things worse.
- Ignore the emotional outburst as much as possible while maintaining pupil safety.
- Avoid direct confrontations.
- Give the pupil time and space to calm down.
- Reassure the pupil afterwards but do not reward them.
- When the pupil has calmed down talk about what upset them in a quiet manner.
- Suggest to the pupil what they could do instead if they feel this way again.

The best way to deal with emotional outbursts is to minimise the likelihood of them happening in the first place: avoid setting up situations where emotional outbursts are likely to happen, e.g. making unrealistic demands or doing complex activities when a pupil is tired; give advance warning, e.g. prepare the pupil for new experiences; give a 5 minute warning that the activity is coming to an end and that you want them to do something else; provide reasonable choices and alternatives to give the pupil a sense of responsibility and control, e.g. choice of activity to do next; choice of materials and encourage the pupil to express their feelings in more positive ways. (See above section on encouraging pupils to recognise and deal with feelings.)

 Key Task

- Outline your school's policy for dealing with a pupil's emotional outburst.
- Describe how *you* have dealt with a pupil's emotional outburst.
- Give examples of opportunities in your school which allow pupils to experience and express their feelings safely.

NOS Links:

Level 2:   **STL 2.2**   **STL 3.4**   **STL 4.1**   **STL 4.3**

Helping pupils to deal with conflict situations

All pupils will experience situations where they feel that life is not fair. They will have disagreements and disputes with other pupils. Initially children rely on adults to help resolve these disputes, but gradually they learn how to deal with these for themselves. Pupils need to learn how to use language to reach agreements so that as far as possible their needs and other people's can be met fairly. Pupils need to learn that resolving conflicts does not mean getting your own way all the time (being aggressive) or allowing others to get their own way all the time (being submissive/passive). There is a better way that allows everyone to reach a satisfactory compromise – being **assertive**.

 key words

Assertive: behaving in a way which is neither passive nor aggressive which allows everyone involved to discuss their feelings/opinions and then negotiate to reach a satisfactory compromise.

Ways to resolve conflicts

Fight/Bully = Aggressive ➔ 'I win so you lose'.

Submit/Retreat = Submissive/Passive ➔ 'I lose because you win'.

Discuss/Negotiate = Assertive ➔ 'I win and you win'.

Some adults may find it difficult to communicate effectively with others, e.g. those with hearing impairment or physical disabilities affecting their ability to articulate sounds. Some parents may speak little or no English. Teaching assistants who have additional communication skills may be very useful in the school, e.g. being able to use sign language to communicate with an adult who has a hearing impairment or bilingual teaching assistants who can liaise with parents whose community language is not English. Teaching assistants who share local community languages may help parents and carers to feel more welcome in the school and help to avoid possible misinterpretations concerning cultural differences.

Sharing information is an essential part of working with pupils and their parents or carers. Adults working with pupils need essential information *from* parents including:

- **Routine information**, e.g. medical history/conditions such as allergies; cultural or religious practices which may have implications for the care and education of the pupil such as special diets, exclusion from RE and assemblies; who collects the pupil (if applicable) including the transport arrangements (such as taxi or minibus) for a pupil with special needs.
- **Emergency information**, e.g. contact telephone numbers for parents/carers, GP.
- **Other information**, e.g. factors which may adversely affect the pupil's behaviour in the school including family difficulties and crises such as divorce, serious illness or bereavement.

Remember to pass on information from parents to the relevant member of staff. Always remember confidentiality with regard to information provided by parents or carers (see below).

Adults working with pupils will also need to *give* parents information on:

- the main aims and objectives of the school
- age range of pupils
- class sizes and staff to pupil ratios
- staff names, roles and qualifications
- school hours and term dates/school holidays
- admission and settling in procedures
- record keeping and assessment
- test/examination targets and results
- an outline of approaches to learning (e.g. the National Curriculum)
- the facilities for indoor and outdoor play including arrangements for swimming
- arrangements for pupils with special needs, including the administration of medicines
- school discipline and behaviour management including rewards and sanctions used
- school procedures regarding food, drink, meal/snack times
- rules regarding school uniform, dress code and jewellery.

 key words

Ratios: the numbers of adults in relation to children within a group setting, e.g. three adults with a group of thirty children would be shown as a ratio of 1:10.

This information is usually given to parents and carers in the play setting's brochure, prospectus or information pack. Information can also be given to parents and carers via letters, notice boards, newsletters and open days.

Key Task

- Give examples of how your school shares information with parents.
- Get a copy of the school's brochure, prospectus or information pack.
- What are your school's policy and procedures for parents wishing to discuss their child's progress with a teacher?

NOS Links:

Level 2:   **STL 4.4**   **STL 12.3**

Sharing information with colleagues

You will be working as part of a team with other professionals including other teaching assistants, teachers and SENCO. Your colleagues will need regular information about your work, e.g. feedback about play and learning activities as well as updates about pupil participation and/or developmental progress. Some of this information may be given orally, for example outlining a pupil's participation and developmental progress during a particular learning activity or commenting on a child's behaviour. Even spoken information needs to be given in a professional manner, e.g. to the appropriate person (the teacher), in the right place (not in a corridor where confidential information could be overheard) and at the right time (urgent matters need to be discussed with the teacher immediately while others may wait until a team meeting). Some information will be in written form, e.g. activity plans, notice boards, newsletters, staff bulletins and records.

Confidentiality matters

Confidentiality is important with regard to sharing information. Only the appropriate people should have access to confidential records. Except where a pupil is potentially at risk, information should not be given to other adults or agencies unless previously agreed. Where the passing of confidential information is acceptable then it should be given in the agreed format. You must always follow the school's policy and procedures regarding confidentiality and the sharing of information. Check with the class teacher or head teacher if you have any concerns about these matters. You should also be aware of any legal requirements with regard to record keeping and accessing information in your school, e.g. Data Protection Act.

The basic provisions of the Data Protection Act

Under the Data Protection Act 1998 all settings processing personal information must comply with the eight enforceable principles of good practice. Personal data must be:

- fairly and lawfully processed
- processed for limited purposes
- adequate, relevant and not excessive
- accurate
- not kept longer than necessary
- processed in accordance with the data subject's rights
- secure
- not transferred to countries without adequate protection.

- **Developing positive working relationships with adults.**
- **Communicating with adults** including: sharing information with parents and carers; sharing information with colleagues.
- **Confidentiality matters** including: the basic provisions of the Data Protection Act; the school's requirements regarding confidentiality.
- **Handling disagreements with other adults**.

Further reading:

Brierley, D. and Treml, G. (eds) (2008) *The Support Staff Little Pocket Book*. 2nd edition. QGP.

DCSF (2008) *Information Sharing: Guidance for Practitioners and Managers*. DCSF & Communities and Local Government. [Available free at: **http://www.teachernet.gov.uk/_doc/13023/isgpm.pdf**]

DfES (2004) *Every Child Matters: Change for Children*. DfES [Available free online at: **http://www.dcsf.gov.uk/everychildmatters/**]

Harvey, N. (2006) *Effective Communication*. 2nd revised edition. Gill & MacMillan Ltd.

Hobart, C. and Frankel, J. (2003) *A Practical Guide to Working with Parents*. Nelson Thornes.

Ramsey, R. D. (2002) *How to Say the Right Thing Every Time: Communicating Well with Students, Staff, Parents and the Public*. Corwin Press.

4. Supporting equality, diversity and inclusion

This chapter relates to QCF unit:

TDA 2.4 Equality, diversity and inclusion in work with children and young people

Understanding children's needs and rights

The principles and values of equality, diversity and inclusion should underpin all work with children. Article 2 of the United Nations Convention on the Rights of the Child requires that children are 'protected from all forms of discrimination'. The Common Core of Skills and Knowledge for the children's workforce sets out common values for those working with children, young people and families that promote equality, respect diversity and challenge stereotypes (Griffin, 2008).

In the past decade there has been a major shift in attitude toward children's rights. Previously children's rights were mainly concerned with children's basic welfare needs. Now, as well as their basic rights to life, health and education, children are viewed as having a much wider range of rights including the right to engage in play activities, to express their views and to participate in making decisions that affect them directly.

Children's rights, as stated in the UN Convention on the Rights of the Child, are clear and universal: they apply to all children. Also, while individual children's needs may differ, they all have the same rights. Children's rights are based on their needs, but emphasising rights rather than needs demonstrates a commitment to viewing and respecting children as valued citizens. (The Children's Rights Alliance for England: **www.crae.org.uk/**.)

All children are special and unique; *all* children have individual needs because they perceive the world differently and interact with others in different ways. All children (including identical twins) have different life experiences which affect their view of the world. Children experience different social and environmental factors which along with their genetic differences shape

key words

Children's needs: these include basic welfare needs such as food, shelter and physical care as well as communication and interaction with others; in addition, educational needs are also important, e.g. opportunities for play and learning which are appropriate for each child's age/level of development.

Children's rights: the universal entitlements to life, health, education, play and consultation which applies to *all* children aged 0 to 18 years.

5. Understanding schools as organisations

This chapter relates to QCF unit:

TDA 2.5 Schools as organisations

The education system in the UK

Free full-time education is available and is compulsory for all children aged 5 to 16 years in the UK. In addition, free education is available for all 3 to 4 year olds whose parents want it, but is not compulsory except in Northern Ireland where compulsory education starts at 4 years old. Pupils are encouraged to continue their education to 18 years either in sixth forms, further education institutions or work-based learning (e.g. apprenticeships) but at the moment this is not compulsory. However, the Education and Skills Act 2008 plans to raise the school leaving age to 18 by 2015.

The state and private sectors in education

In the UK education is provided by both the state and private sectors. Parents may choose to send their children to schools in the state or private sector or they can educate their children by any approved suitable means, e.g. home schooling. State or maintained schools are funded by the government with no direct financial contribution by parents. State schools are mostly comprehensive in that they accept pupils of all academic abilities; they are also co-educational meaning they have both boys and girls. In some areas there are still grammar schools which select the more academically able pupils and these tend to be single sex. Many state-funded secondary schools are specialist schools which receive extra funding for providing one or more specialist subject, e.g. computing, music, science, sport. Nearly all state schools are day schools, although there are a few state-funded boarding schools where the education is paid for by the government but the boarding fees are paid by parents. Some state-funded schools are faith schools such as Christian (mostly Catholic or Church of England) and Jewish, Muslim or Hindu.

The private sector consists of independent or public schools where fees are paid by parents. Most of these are boarding schools although some are day schools. Some boarding schools also include day pupils and weekly boarders (pupils who go home every weekend).

Types of schools

In the UK there are many different types of schools and other education settings for children aged 0 to 18 years. These can be organised into four main phases of education:

1. **Pre-school and nursery education** (0 to 5 year olds) includes: pre-school groups, playgroups, nursery centres, day nurseries, nursery schools, pupils aged 4–5 years in reception classes in primary schools.
2. **Primary education** (5 to 11 year olds) includes: primary schools, infant schools, junior schools, first schools, pupils aged 4–5 years in primary schools in Northern Ireland, pupils aged 8–11 years in middle schools, pupils aged 11–12 years in lower secondary education in Scotland.
3. **Secondary education** (11 to 16 year olds) includes: secondary schools, pupils aged 11–13 years in middle schools, high schools, grammar schools, academies, city technology colleges, pupils aged 12–16 years in lower secondary education in Scotland.
4. **Further education** (16 to 18 year olds) includes: school sixth forms, sixth form centres/ colleges, FE colleges, tertiary colleges, specialist colleges, pupils aged 16–18 years in upper secondary education in Scotland.

Some schools may include several education phases in one setting, e.g. special schools for pupils with special needs aged 0 to 18 years.

 **Activity!**

- What type of school or other education setting do you work in?
- What are the ages of pupils you work with?

The school workforce

The school workforce consists of qualified teachers and support staff.

- Qualified teachers in the leadership group, e.g. head teachers, deputy or assistant head teachers and other qualified teachers.
- Classroom teachers including Qualified Teacher Status (QTS) e.g. newly or recently qualified teachers; Core Teachers – teachers on the main pay scale; Post Threshold Teachers – teachers on the upper pay scale; Excellent Teachers; Advanced Skills Teachers.
- Support staff including learning support staff, e.g. Teaching Assistants, Higher Level Teaching Assistants, Nursery Nurses, Sports Technicians/Assistants and Cover Supervisors;
- Pupil support/welfare staff, e.g. Learning Mentors, Play Workers, Midday Supervisors, Parent Support Advisors.
- Administrative staff, e.g. School Business Managers, Administrative Assistants, Secretaries, Examination Officers.
- Specialist technicians and assistants, e.g. Librarians and Library Assistants, Information and Communication Tecnology Technicians/Assistants, Design and Technology Technicians/ Assistants, Food Technicians, Science Technicians.
- Site staff e.g. Cleaners, Catering Staff and Cooks, Site/Premises Managers and Caretakers.

(For more information about support staff roles in schools visit the TDA website: **http://www. tda.gov.uk/support/support_staff_roles.aspx**.)

You must know and follow the setting's policies and procedures for maintaining child safety at all times especially during play and learning activities including outings. It is important to provide challenging and exciting play and learning activities that encourage children to develop and explore whilst still maintaining their physical safety and emotional welfare.

(Information about statutory and regulatory health and safety requirements can be found in Chapter 2.)

 **Activity!**

Find out about your school's policy and procedures for health and safety.

Risk assessment applicable to the learning environment

You must know and understand the importance of pupils being given opportunities to play and learn within an environment that will not harm their health and safety. Adult supervision should be provided as appropriate to the ages/levels of development of the children (e.g. very young children need close supervision with a high adult:child ratio). As children grow and develop their physical abilities they need to be provided with activities and experiences that have levels of challenge and risk that will help them to develop confidence and independence.

You need to be able to identify potential **hazards** (e.g. activities likely to cause harm) and assess possible **risks** (e.g. the seriousness of the hazards and their potential to cause actual harm).

key words

Hazards: activities likely to cause harm.

Risks: the seriousness of the hazards and their potential to cause actual harm.

Risk assessment: a systematic review of the potential for harm including identifying hazards, evaluating possible risks, evaluating existing control measures and specifying any further action.

1. The purpose of **risk assessment** is to: undertake a systematic review of the potential for harm; evaluate the likelihood of harm occurring; decide whether the existing control measures are adequate; and decide whether more needs to be done.
2. The sequence for risk assessment is: classify the activity; identify potential hazard(s); evaluate possible risks; evaluate control measures; and specify any further action.
3. Once the risk assessment has been carried out, the hierarchy for control measures is: eliminate hazard; reduce hazard; isolate hazard; and control hazard.
4. Once the risk assessment and control measures have been completed no further action needs to be taken unless there is a significant change in that area.

(RoSPA, 2004b)

 **Activity!**

Outline the procedures for risk assessment and dealing with hazards in your school.

You must know and understand the basic stages of child development and the implications these have for health, safety and security arrangements. For detailed information go to the Child Accident Prevention Trust (CAPT) website: **www.capt.org.uk** and then clink 'Downloads' to access free samples of these aged-related safety leaflets:

- *Handle safely: babies from birth to crawling*
- *Active steps to safety: toddlers up to the age of 5*
- *Step safely with a helping hand: children aged 5 to 7*
- *Step safely from the edge: children aged 7 to 11*
- *It's a safety thing: young people aged 11 to 14.*

Remember that despite the school's procedures to maintain children's safety, there may still be times when accidents or injuries occur. Ensure that you know how to deal with accidents and injuries as well as the arrangements for first aid. (See section below on dealing with accidents and injuries.)

Figure 6.1: Pupil wearing safety goggles

 **Activity!**

Find out about the particular safety implications for the pupils you work with.

Checking equipment is safe for use

All equipment in the school should be safe and approved for safety, e.g. BSI Kitemark, European standards markings, or BEAB mark of safety. You should know the operating procedures and safety requirements of the school before using any equipment. Operating instructions should be available and in many cases an experienced/knowledgeable member of staff may show you how to use the equipment beforehand. If not, it is essential to ask, especially when dealing with electrical equipment, for safety reasons and the possibility of damaging expensive equipment – you do not want to causes hundreds or even thousands of pounds worth of damage to a computer or photocopier! You should follow any instructions carefully. Allow yourself plenty of time to do this thoroughly. Five minutes before you need to show the group/class a DVD is not the time to start learning how to use the school's DVD player for the first time! As with all learning activities you must plan ahead.

You should check equipment that you use regularly to ensure that it is safe and in proper working order, for example, check the television, video or computer is in working order before you or the pupils need it so that you can sort out any problems in advance. If there is a fault and the equipment is not functioning properly or not at all you need to know the appropriate school procedures for dealing with faults, for example, which can be dealt with by you and which require reporting to the appropriate person. It is also important to check classroom equipment and materials regularly for damage and to report any damage to the appropriate person such as the class or subject teacher. Serious damage will have to be repaired by a professional (e.g. a technician or the school caretaker) or the item will have to be replaced.

Storing materials and equipment safely

Storage areas should be kept tidy with sufficient space for the materials and equipment being stored there. Storage facilities should be easily accessible and, where appropriate, lockable. Potentially hazardous materials must be stored away from pupils and locked away. Storage space should be organised so that heavy equipment is stored at a low level. Lightweight equipment may be stored above head-level if space is limited. One of your responsibilities as a teaching assistant may be to ensure that all equipment and surfaces are safe, hygienic and usable. If working with pupils who have been using messy materials such as glue or paint, you will need to wipe tables or easels clean after use and clean any brushes ready for the next time. Any major cleaning tasks that are not part of your responsibilities should be referred to the class or subject teacher for attention. It is also important to ensure proper hygiene and correct use of equipment. For example, using fresh ingredients when doing cooking activities and ensuring pupils wash their hands before and after, or following the correct procedures during science experiments.

Ten important safety points to remember

Remember the following important safety points when establishing a healthy, safe and secure learning environment:

1. All equipment and materials must be appropriate to the ages/levels of development of the pupils, for example, small items are potential choking hazards for young children.

2. Pupils must listen carefully and follow instructions on the use of equipment and materials during activities, e.g. handling fragile or breakable objects with care.

3. Pupils must be told never to put anything in their mouths during learning activities unless instructed to do so by the adult in charge (e.g. they may be allowed to sample food during a cooking or tasting activity).

4. Safety goggles to British Standard BS2092 (that can also be worn with spectacles) should be worn by pupils engaged in potentially hazardous activities such as sawing, hammering and science experiments involving chemicals.

5. Pupils should not touch electrical equipment, especially with wet hands.

6. When pupils are doing cooking activities ensure that: ingredients are fresh and in good condition; dried ingredients are stored in airtight containers; cooking utensils and table surfaces are scrupulously clean; and all hands are washed beforehand.

7. Check if any pupil is prevented from taking part in an activity due to cultural or religious dietary prohibitions; ensure that individual children are not allergic to any of the ingredients or materials.

8. Long hair should be tied back during construction, cooking, PE and science activities.

9. Pupils should be taught how to use, arrange and store PE apparatus correctly and safely as appropriate to their age and level of development.

10. Pupils should report all accidents to the teacher or teaching assistant.

 **Activity!**

List 10 important safety points to remember when organising classroom resources.

Nikki works at Parkside After-School Club and has started to complete a risk assessment for the outdoor play area. She has used the key below to estimate the Risk (R) by multiplying (X) the Severity (S) by the Likelihood (L) S × L = R

Complete the risk assessment with more examples from your own workplace.

Hazard	Who is at risk?	Severity	Likelihood	Risk estimate = S × L	Controls needed
Entry/exit gates left open	Children	3	2	6	Outside gates locked Constant supervision
Hedging/plants	Children, adults	1	2	2	Cut back hedging regularly
Skipping ropes – tripping	Children	1	2	2	Regular supervision
Footballs – being hit, breakages	Children, adults	1	2	2	Provide sufficient space for games
Sunburn	Children, adults	2	2	4	Provide sun hats Parents/carers to put cream on children

Hazard severity
3 Major
2 Serious
1 Slight

Hazard likelihood
3 High = certain harm will occur
2 Medium = could occur frequently
1 Low = seldom occurs

Figure 6.2: Risk assessment form

Maintaining toilet and wash areas

It is important that toilet and wash facilities are maintained in a clean and orderly condition with adequate lighting and ventilation. For children over two years old there should be one toilet and hand basin for every ten children. There should be separate toilet facilities for pupils and staff. There should be an adequate supply of drinking water that is easily accessible to pupils. The school should ensure that toilet facilities are maintained to high standards of hygiene. There should be adequate supplies of toilet paper, soap, warm water and disposable paper towels and/ or access to hot air driers. The cleaning routines for toilets and washbasins should be regular and thorough to maintain high standards of hygiene. To minimise the spread of infection, the school should advise parents whose children have diarrhoea that the children should stay away from the setting until they no longer have symptoms. Your role might involve checking pupil toilet areas to see that they are used correctly and that pupils wash their hands after using the toilet or before handling food. You may be required to assist very young pupils (or pupils with physical disabilities) with their toileting needs. You should know the school's procedures for dealing with pupils who wet or soil themselves including the location of appropriate spare clothing.

You may need to provide reassurance and support for a girl who starts menstruation but does not have any sanitary protection. (Girls as young as 8 or 9 can start their first period while at the setting.) You should know the school's procedures for dealing with this situation, including accessing emergency supplies of sanitary protection and its disposal. If you are a male teaching assistant then you must know who to go to for help if this situation occurs.

If you experience any concerns or problems with pupils when carrying out hygiene routines, you should report these to the class teacher. This includes reporting any hazard or unsafe situation you discover when using the school's toilet or wash facilities.

 **Activity!**

What are your school's procedures for checking toilet and wash areas? What are your responsibilities in checking these areas?

Play areas and playgrounds

Accidents are common in children because they are developing and learning rapidly and it can be difficult for adults to keep up with their changing developmental abilities. Accidents also occur because children are naturally curious and want to explore their environment and in doing so may expose themselves to danger. The setting should provide play and learning activities that encourage child curiosity and exploration whilst protecting them from unnecessary harm. Children also need to learn how to deal with risk so that they can keep themselves safe as they grow up. Bumps, bruises, minor cuts and scrapes are all part of play and learning but there is no need for children to suffer serious injuries. To avoid accidents the setting should provide adult care and supervision as well as ensuring safe play equipment design and appropriate modifications to the learning environment (CAPT, 2004a).

The design, location and maintenance of play areas are important to maintaining child safety during play and learning activities. It is essential to remember the following:

- The layout must ensure that activities in one area do not interfere with other areas.
- Play areas for younger children should be separated from those for older children.
- Paths must be safely situated away from equipment areas, especially swings.
- Clear sight lines in the play area make it easier to supervise children.
- Secure fencing is required if there are roads, rivers or ponds close to the play area.
- Safe access for children with disabilities should be considered.
- Lighting must be adequate for safety and supervision.
- Old or worn play equipment should be repaired or replaced.
- Play equipment should be suitable for the age of the children using it.
- Impact-absorbing surfaces such as rubber, bark chips and other materials should be used.

(CAPT, 2004b)

Making sure that children are aware of safe behaviour when using play equipment can also help to maintain their safety and protect them from unnecessary accidents. Examples of safe behaviour include:

- No walking in front of swings or other moving equipment.
- No pushing or shoving; being aware of younger children and those with disabilities.
- Removing scarves or other things that could get caught in equipment.
- Taking extra care when using high play equipment such as climbing frames.

(CAPT, 2004b)

There is a duty under Sections 3 and 4 of the Health and Safety at Work Act 1974 to ensure the health and safety of users of playground equipment as far as is reasonably practicable (RoSPA, 2004a). Evidence of good practice in ensuring the health and safety of users includes compliance with the relevant safety standards, for example EN 1176 for children's playground equipment and EN 1177 for playground surfaces.

Safety checks for indoor play areas and outdoor play areas/playgrounds include:

1. Inspecting the play area/playground equipment on a regular basis.
2. Reporting any faults to the appropriate person promptly.
3. Ensuring that children do not use the faulty equipment until mended or replaced.
4. Getting the necessary repairs done as quickly as possible.
5. Having an annual inspection by an independent specialist.

Toy safety

Toy safety is also an essential aspect of maintaining child safety. Every year in the UK over 35,000 children under the age of 15 years are treated in hospital following an accident involving a toy (CAPT, 2002). It is essential to provide children with toys and play equipment that are appropriate for their ages and levels of development. Most toys will have a suggested age range. It is a legal requirement for all toys sold in the European Union to carry a CE mark but this does not necessarily guarantee safety or quality. When selecting toys for children always look for one of these safety marks –

Figure 6.3: Toy safety

European Standard BS EN 71 (indicates the toy has been tested to the agreed safety standards) or the *Lion Mark* (indicates the toy has been made to the highest standards of safety and quality).

The movement and activity of pupils

You also need to consider the safety of children and adults when entering and exiting the setting as well as their movement and activity while in the setting. Schools cater for the arrival and departure of children, families, workers and visitors either as pedestrians or in vehicles, including delivery vans and taxis for pupils with special needs. Traffic routes should be properly organised so that both pedestrians and vehicles can move safely in and around the school. Particular care should be taken of everyone using or having access to the premises especially young children and people with disabilities. The school may have to cope with the large-scale movement of pupils and staff during busy periods, for example, the start and finish of lessons. Care should be taken to avoid accidents such as slips, trips or falls particularly in main corridors and staircases. Floor surfaces should be appropriate for their use and free from hazards or obstructions that might cause people to trip or fall. Particular attention should be given to: holes, bumps and uneven surfaces; wear and tear on carpeted areas; procedures for dealing with spillages; snow and ice on external pathways and precautionary measures prior to repairs, e.g. barriers, alternative routes.

Security arrangements for pupil arrival and departure

You must know and follow the school's policy and procedures for gaining access to the premises, e.g. entry systems, visitors' book, identity tags for visitors in the school. Security arrangements should include a registration system, e.g. a record of the time of arrival and departure of pupils and staff; a visitors' book to record name of visitor, who they are/who they work for, time of arrival, who they are visiting, car registration if applicable, and time of departure. Anyone visiting the school for the first time should provide proof of identity. Pupils should never be left unattended with an adult who is not a member of staff.

A pupil must not be allowed to leave the school with an adult who does not usually collect the pupil without prior permission. You should also know and follow your school's policy and procedures for uncollected pupils or late arrival of parent or carer to collect younger pupils.

 **Activity!**

- Find out about your setting's policy and procedures for gaining access to the premises.
- Find out about your setting's policy and procedures for uncollected children.

Following procedures for missing pupils

A register of pupils attending each class in the school should be taken at the start of each session. A register should also be taken for pupils participating in outings/visits away from the school with a duplicate left with the head teacher. Pupils should be made aware (or reminded) of the boundaries of the school at each session. Pupils should be appropriately supervised at all times. However, despite these safeguards pupils may still go missing from the school. You need to be aware of the school's procedures for dealing with missing pupils. These procedures may include: contacting the class teacher or head teacher immediately; calling the register to check which pupil is missing; searching classrooms, play areas and school grounds to ensure the pupil has not hidden or been locked in anywhere within the school and the head teacher contacting the police and the parent/carers.

If a pupil is found to be missing while on an outing the teaching assistant should: contact the class teacher immediately; check the register again; keep the rest of the group together while searching the area and contact the class teacher again (who will contact the head teacher, the police and the pupil's parents/carers).

 **Activity!**

Briefly outline your school's procedures for dealing with missing pupils.

Key Task

1. Outline your school's policies and procedures for maintaining health and safety.
2. What are your responsibilities for dealing with the following types of possible hazards that can occur in the school:
   - unsafe buildings, fixtures and fittings
   - unsafe equipment including play and learning resources
   - hazardous substances, e.g. cleaning materials
   - hygiene hazards in toilet or kitchen areas
   - security hazards, e.g. inadequate boundaries, unauthorised visitors?

NOS LINKS:

Level 2:   STL3.1   STL10.5   STL13.1   STL13.2

Following emergency evacuation procedures in the school

You need to know about the fire and emergency evacuation procedures for the school. The purpose of fire and emergency evacuation procedures is to prevent panic and to ensure the safe, orderly and efficient evacuation of all occupants of the school using all the exit facilities available and to help individuals to react rationally when confronted with a fire or other emergency either at the school or elsewhere. *In the event of a fire or other emergency (such as a bomb scare) all staff should know and understand that their first consideration must be the evacuation of all the pupils to a place of safety.*

The sequence for fire and emergency evacuation procedures should be as follows:

1. Sound the fire alarm.
2. Evacuate the building.
3. Call the fire brigade.
4. Assemble at the designated assembly point.
5. Take a roll call using registers if possible.

The fire alarm signals the need to evacuate the building. You should give calm, clear and correct instructions to the people involved in the emergency as appropriate to your role in implementing emergency procedures within the school. You will need to make sure that any pupils for whom you are responsible leave the building in the appropriate manner, e.g. walking, no running or talking. This will help to maintain calm and minimise panic as the pupils focus on following the appropriate evacuation procedures. All rooms must have evacuation instructions, including exit routes, prominently displayed.

Figure 6.4: Fire evacuation instructions

Key Task

1. Find out about your school's procedures for: dealing with accidents and injuries; providing first aid.
2. Describe your role and responsibilities in the event of an accident, injury, illness or other emergency situation.

NOS Links:

Level 2:   STL 3.2

Summary of key points in this unit:

- **Maintaining health and safety during play and learning activities** including: risk assessment applicable to the learning environment; checking equipment is safe for use; storing materials and equipment safely; maintaining toilet and wash areas; play areas and playgrounds; toy safety; the movement and activity of pupils; security arrangements for pupil arrival and departure; following procedures for missing pupils.
- **Following emergency evacuation procedures in the school** including fire and emergency evacuation procedures as well as what to do in the event of a bomb scare or an intruder in the school.
- **Dealing with accidents and injuries** including following first aid arrangements and first aid equipment.

Further reading

Dare, A. and O'Donovan, M. (2000) *Good Practice in Child Safety*. Nelson Thornes.

DfEE (1998) *Guidance on First Aid for Settings: A Good Practice Guide*. Department for Education and Employment.

DfEE (1998) *Health and Safety of Children on Educational Visits: A Good Practice Guide*. DfEE.

DfES (2004) *Every Child Matters: Change for Children. DfES*. Available free online at: **http://www.dcsf.gov. uk/everychildmatters/about/.**

HSE (2005) *COSHH: A Brief Guide to the Regulations: What You Need to Know about the Control of Substances Hazardous to Health Regulations 2002*. Leaflet INDG136 (rev3). HSE Books.

HSE (2006) *Five Steps to Risk Assessment*. INDG163 (rev2). HSE Books.

HSE (2006) *Health and Safety Law: What You Should Know*. Leaflet. HSE Books.

St. John Ambulance, St. Andrew's Ambulance Association and British Red Cross (2009) *First Aid Manual: The Step by Step Guide for Everyone*. 9th edition. Penguin.

[Note: Single copies of the above HSE leaflets are available free from: **www.hse.gov.uk**]

7. Supporting learning activities

This chapter relates to QCF unit:

TDA 2.10 Support learning activities

Understanding pupil development and learning

An understanding of intellectual development is essential for teaching assistants because it helps them to assist the teacher in supporting learning activities through: a well-organised and structured learning environment; careful planning and preparation of learning activities; the provision of appropriate learning resources; effective communication with pupils during learning activities; high adult expectations for learner development and accurate evaluation of learning activities and assessment of pupil abilities.

How children think and learn

Research into how children think and learn has made adults more aware of the need to: observe and assess children's development very carefully; listen to children and the way they express ideas and take account of children's interests and experiences when planning learning opportunities. Here we look at some of the main theories relating to the development of cognitive skills – Piaget, Vygotsky and Bruner.

key words

Cognitive: intellectual abilities involving processing information received through the senses.

Schemas: term used mainly by Piaget and Froebel to describe internal thought processes.

Piaget, a Swiss biologist, used observations of his own children, plus a wider sample of children, to develop his theories of cognitive development. Piaget's theories of cognitive development have had a major influence on early education for over 40 years. Piaget believed that children went through different *stages* of cognitive development based on fixed ages. Within these stages the children's patterns of learning, or schemas as he called them, were very different from adult ways of problem-solving.

Piaget also believed in the importance of young children learning through action and exploration of their environment using their sensory motor skills. According to Piaget, children are *actively* involved in structuring their own cognitive development through exploration of their environment. Children need real objects and 'concrete experiences' to discover things for themselves. The adult's role is to provide children with appropriate experiences in a suitable environment to facilitate the children's instinctive ability to think and learn. Cognitive development occurs in four set stages which are universal – they apply to all forms of learning and across all cultures.

Bruner views language as central to children's thinking and learning and stresses how language is used to represent experiences and how past experience or knowledge is organised through language in ways which make information more accessible. Language connects a person's understanding of one situation to another. The adult has a particular role in establishing effective communication to encourage and extend children's thinking and learning. Adults use language to: capture children's interest and direct their attention; develop children's problem-solving abilities; assist children's understanding of concepts; encourage and extend children's own ideas and negotiate choices with children.

Activity!

Make a list of the main points of Piaget's, Vygotsky's and Bruner's theories concerning children's thinking and learning. Think about how these ideas relate to your experiences of working with pupils.

Learning experiences

Every learning experience can be viewed as a journey, travelling along different pathways to reach our destination or learning goal (Drummond, 1994). At different points of a learning experience the learning may be:

- very easy – speeding along a clear motorway
- interesting, but uncertain in parts – taking the scenic route
- very difficult and complicated – stuck in a traffic jam on spaghetti junction

Figure 7.2: Adult supporting children engaged in writing activity

- totally confusing – trying to find the correct exit from a big road traffic island
- completely beyond us – entering a no-through road or going the wrong way down a one-way street.

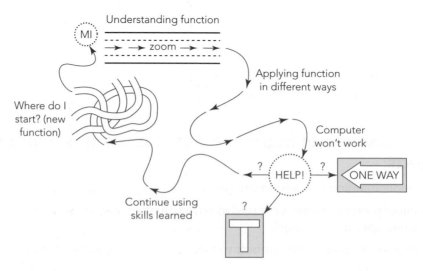

Figure 7.3: Learning pathways

 **Activity!**

Think about your own experiences of learning:
- as an adult (e.g. learning to drive, cook, study; becoming a teaching assistant)
- as a child (e.g. learning to tie shoe laces, read, ride a bike, swim).

Draw diagrams to show your learning pathways or journeys. Your pictures might look something like the diagram in Figure 7.3.

Patterns of learning

The experience of learning is a never-ending cycle; learning new skills continues indefinitely. Once one skill is gained in a particular area, further skills can be learned. For example, once pupils have learned basic reading skills, they continue to develop their literacy skills even as adults by increasing their vocabulary, improving their spelling, decoding unfamiliar words and reading and understanding more complex texts.

 **Activity!**

Think about the learning experiences of the pupils in your school. Select two pupils and draw diagrams of their learning experiences. Compare them with your own experiences of learning. Are there any similarities or differences?

As well as the circular nature of learning experiences, you may also have noticed the importance of *active participation* in all learning experiences. Watching someone else use a computer or read a book can only help so much – to develop the relevant skills, people need hands-on experience of using the computer or handling books.

Active learning

Active participation is essential in all effective learning experiences. **Active learning** is an important part of all learning experiences – not just for children but for adults as well. For example, at college or school you may find that learning situations take the form of workshops, group activities and discussions rather than formal lectures.

 **key words**

Active learning: learning by doing; participation in activities in meaningful situations.

It is essential that pupils become actively involved in the learning process. Learning needs to be practical not theoretical. Pupils need concrete learning experiences, that is, using real objects in a meaningful context. Children (and adults) learn by doing. In all learning situations it is important to provide information in small portions with plenty of discussion and activity breaks to maintain interest and concentration. This is because the average attention span of a child is about 5 to 10 minutes and can be as little as 2 to 3 minutes.

Play is an essential part of the active learning process. Through active learning, pupils use play opportunities to encourage and extend the problem-solving abilities that are essential to developing their intellectual processes. Play activities provide informal opportunities for pupils to develop ideas and to understand concepts through active learning and communication. (See section on the role of play in children's learning and development in Chapter 11.)

Figure 7.4: Pupils engaged in active learning

Learning styles

Pupils have different ways of processing information. Pupils use the skills of looking, listening or touching in varying amounts depending on their individual learning style. For example, some pupils require visual stimulation; some respond well to verbal instructions while others need more 'hands on' experiences. In addition, different times of the day affect individual levels of concentration; some pupils work better in the morning, others in the afternoon. You need to be aware of the individual learning styles of the pupils you work with in order to plan and provide appropriate learning activities. Recognising learning styles will help you to understand the ways pupils learn and to assist them in achieving educational success.

<u>Visual learners</u> gather information through observation and reading. Pupils with this learning style may find it difficult to concentrate on spoken instructions, but respond well to visual aids such as pictures, diagrams and charts. They tend to visualise ideas and remember the visual details of places and objects they have seen. According to research about 65 per cent of people have this learning style.

<u>Auditory learners</u> process information by listening carefully and then repeating instructions either out loud or mentally in order to remember what they have learned. Research suggests that about 30 per cent of people use this style of learning. Pupils with this learning style tend to be the talkers as well as the listeners in group and/or class situations and benefit from being able to discuss ideas. Auditory learners can be easily distracted by noise and may concentrate better with background music to disguise potentially disruptive noises.

 key words

Auditory learners: process information by listening carefully and then repeating instructions either out loud or mentally in order to remember what they have learned; they benefit from being able to discuss ideas.

Kinaesthetic learners: process information through touch and movement e.g. active learning; they benefit from physical interaction with their environment with plenty of emphasis on learning by doing.

Visual learners: gather information through observation and reading by remembering the visual details of things they have seen; they benefit from visual aids such as pictures, diagrams and charts.

<u>Kinaesthetic learners</u> process information through touch and movement. All young children rely on this learning style to a large extent hence the importance of active learning (see below)

especially in the early years. About 5 per cent of people continue to use this style even as adults. Pupils with this learning style will benefit from physical interaction with their environment with plenty of emphasis on learning by doing.

Pupils are not restricted to learning in only one way as they can learn to use different learning styles for different activities within the curriculum. However, research shows that working outside their preferred learning style for extensive periods can be stressful. Providing opportunities for pupils to use their preferred learning style, wherever practical, increases their chances of educational success (Tobias, 1996).

As well as relying on one particular style of learning, people also tend to use one of two styles of processing information: either analytic or global. **Analytic learners** process information by dividing it into pieces and organising it in a logical manner, e.g. making lists, putting things in order, following clear instructions or rules and completing/handing in work on time. Analytic learners prefer order and a planned, predictable sequence of events or ideas. **Global learners** process information by grouping large pieces of information together and focusing on the main ideas rather than details, e.g. drawing spider-grams, using pictures or key words, ignoring or bending rules including missing deadlines. Global learners prefer spontaneity and activities which allow them creative freedom.

 key words

Analytic learners: process information by dividing it into pieces and organising it in a logical manner e.g. making lists, putting things in order, and following clear instructions or rules.

Global learners: process information by grouping large pieces of information together and focusing on the main ideas rather than details e.g. drawing spider-grams, using pictures or key words.

 **Activity!**

- Think about how the pupil or pupils you work with gather information. Do they prefer to: work as an individual or in a group; follow step-by-step instructions or have open-ended projects; read and talk about work or engage in practical activities and experiment for themselves?
- Think about how the pupils you work with process information. Are they analytic or global learners?

Factors affecting learning

Intellectual development is affected by other factors besides the pupil's chronological age. Factors affecting learning can include: lack of play opportunities; unrewarding learning activities; lack of opportunities to use language and communication skills; inappropriate learning activities; introduction to formal learning situations at too early an age and English as an additional language. Some pupils may not develop their intellectual processes in line with the expected pattern of development for their age due to special needs such as: communication and/or interaction difficulties; learning difficulties; behavioural, social or emotional difficulties (see Chapter 12).

The inability to concentrate, to work independently or to use investigative skills may make it very difficult for some pupils to participate fully in learning activities. This may lead to subsequent learning difficulties in curriculum areas such as English, mathematics, science, technology and so on. Some pupils may be inaccurately thought to have learning difficulties, when they are really experiencing a lack of appropriate intellectual stimulation. Children with little or no intellectual stimulation cannot develop their own thinking skills or formulate new ideas. It is vital that all pupils have access to a stimulating learning environment that enables them to learn in exciting and challenging ways. Intellectual stimulation through appropriate learning activities allows pupils to develop their intellectual abilities and to fulfil their potential as individuals.

Curriculum frameworks

As appropriate to your particular role, you will need to support learning activities within the curriculum frameworks for education for your home country: England, Northern Ireland, Scotland or Wales. For example in England the curriculum frameworks for education are the Early Years Foundation Stage (0 to 5 years) and the National Curriculum Key Stages 1 to 4 (5 to 16 years).

The Early Years Foundation Stage

Orders and regulations under section 39 of the Childcare Act 2006 brought the Early Years Foundation Stage (EYFS) into force in September 2008. All early years providers are required to use the EYFS to ensure a coherent and flexible approach to children's care, learning and development that will enable young children to achieve the five *Every Child Matters* outcomes: staying safe; being healthy; enjoying and achieving; making a positive contribution; and achieving economic well-being (see Chapter 4).

There are six areas covered by the early learning goals and educational programmes. None of these areas can be delivered in isolation from the others. They are equally important and depend on each other to support a rounded approach to child development. All the areas must be delivered through planned, purposeful play, with a balance of adult-led and child-initiated activities. The six areas of learning and development are:

- Personal, Social and Emotional Development
- Communication, Language and Literacy
- Problem Solving, Reasoning and Numeracy
- Knowledge and Understanding of the World
- Physical Development
- Creative Development.

For more information on EYFS see: **http://nationalstrategies.standards.dcsf.gov.uk/earlyyears**.

The National Curriculum

The National Curriculum sets out the statutory requirements for the knowledge and skills that every child is expected to learn in schools. The National Curriculum framework enables teachers to provide all school-aged children with challenging learning experiences, taught in ways that are both balanced and manageable. The National Curriculum sets out the standards to be used to measure the progress and performance of pupils in each subject, to help teachers plan and implement learning activities that meet the individual learning needs of pupils.

The National Curriculum applies to children of compulsory school age in schools in England. The National Curriculum sets out what pupils should study, what they should be taught and the standards that they should achieve. It is divided into four key stages:

- **Key Stage 1:** 5 to 7 year olds (Year groups: 1 and 2)
- **Key Stage 2:** 7 to 11 year olds (Year groups: 3, 4, 5 and 6)
- **Key Stage 3:** 11 to 14 year olds (Year groups: 7, 8 and 9)
- **Key Stage 4:** 14 to 16 year olds (Year groups: 10 and 11).

The primary Curriculum

In Key Stages I and 2 in the National Curriculum the compulsory subjects consist of: English; Mathematics; Science; Information and Communication Technology; Design and Technology; History; Geography; Art and Design; Music and Physical Education. In addition there is a non-statutory framework for Personal, Social and Health Education (PSHE) and Citizenship. Primary schools must also provide Religious Education although parents may withdraw their children from this if they wish to do so. Primary schools must also provide sex education but again parents can withdraw their children from these lessons. From September 2010, the teaching of Modern Foreign Languages will be statutory in Key Stage 2.

For more information see: **http://nationalstrategies.standards.dcsf.gov.uk/primary**.

The secondary Curriculum

In Key Stage 3 in the National Curriculum the compulsory subjects are: English; Mathematics; Science; Information and Communication Technology; Design and Technology; History; Geography; Art and Design; Music; Physical Education, Citizenship and Modern Foreign Languages.

In Key Stage 4 the compulsory subjects are English, Mathematics, Science, Information and Communication Technology, Physical Education and Citizenship. Secondary schools must make entitlement curriculum areas (e.g. the arts, design and technology, the humanities and modern foreign languages) available to all students who wish to study them. In addition, there is a new statutory requirement for work-related learning and a non-statutory framework setting out the minimum experience that schools should provide for work-related learning.

In Key Stages 3 and 4 there is a non-statutory framework for Personal, Social and Health and Economic Education as well as Religious Education, which is a statutory subject with a non-statutory programme of study. As in primary schools, parents may withdraw their children from Religious Education and Sex Education lessons if they wish to do so, except for the aspects of sex education (e.g. human reproduction) included as part of the Science programme of study.

For more information see: **http://nationalstrategies.standards.dcsf.gov.uk/secondary**.

The Diploma is a new qualification for 14 to 19 year olds which offers a mix of academic and practical skills within one of these broad sector-related subject areas: Construction and the Built Environment; Creative and Media; Engineering; Information Technology; Society, Health and Development; Environmental and Land-based Studies; Business, Administration and Finance; Manufacturing and Product Design; Hospitality and Hair and Beauty Studies. From September 2010 the following areas will also be available: Travel and Tourism, Public Services; Sport and Active Leisure and Retail Business. Three more areas will be available from September 2011: Humanities and Social Sciences, Languages and International Communication and Science.

The Diploma does not replace GCSEs or A levels but will be studied alongside compulsory subjects such as English, Mathematics, Science and ICT. The Diploma has three levels of study:

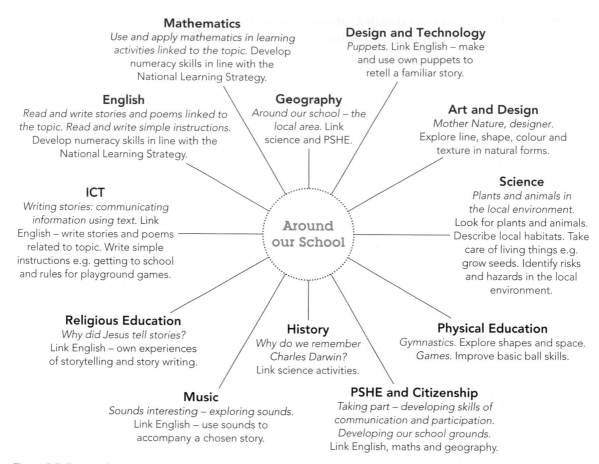

Mathematics
Use and apply mathematics in learning activities linked to the topic. Develop numeracy skills in line with the National Learning Strategy.

Design and Technology
Puppets. Link English – make and use own puppets to retell a familiar story.

English
Read and write stories and poems linked to the topic. Read and write simple instructions. Develop numeracy skills in line with the National Learning Strategy.

Geography
Around our school – the local area. Link science and PSHE.

Art and Design
Mother Nature, designer. Explore line, shape, colour and texture in natural forms.

ICT
Writing stories: communicating information using text. Link English – write stories and poems related to topic. Write simple instructions e.g. getting to school and rules for playground games.

Around our School

Science
Plants and animals in the local environment. Look for plants and animals. Describe local habitats. Take care of living things e.g. grow seeds. Identify risks and hazards in the local environment.

Religious Education
Why did Jesus tell stories? Link English – own experiences of storytelling and story writing.

History
Why do we remember Charles Darwin? Link science activities.

Physical Education
Gymnastics. Explore shapes and space. *Games.* Improve basic ball skills.

Music
Sounds interesting – exploring sounds. Link English – use sounds to accompany a chosen story.

PSHE and Citizenship
Taking part – developing skills of communication and participation. Developing our school grounds. Link English, maths and geography.

Figure 7.5: Topic web

Short-term plans

Short-term plans should be based on the long-term plan and medium-term plans as well as ongoing observations and assessments of pupils including discussions with colleagues and parents. Staff should use this information to plan appropriate activities and experiences for pupils.

Short-term plans provide details of learning activities on a weekly, daily and lesson-by-lesson basis. Planning appropriate learning activities involves: identifying the intended learning outcomes that promote inclusion, participation and achievement for all pupils; using information about pupil interests, skills and prior achievements to structure the content and progress of activities/lessons; taking into account individual learning and development needs including different learning styles (see above); including targets from individual education plans for pupils with special educational needs; defining the roles and responsibilities of the staff involved; insuring that adequate and appropriate resources are available and using ICT to support children's learning and development.

Key Task

Provide examples of the planning you and the teacher(s) use within the curriculum framework applicable to the pupils in your school. Include information on:

- long-term plans, e.g. overall curriculum plan, topic web
- medium-term plans, e.g. schemes of work, timetables
- short-term plans, e.g. activity plans, lesson plans.

NOS Links:

Level 2:   STL 1.1   STL 2.4

Supporting the teacher in the planning of learning activities

As appropriate to your particular role, you will need to support the teacher in planning, delivering and evaluating learning activities according to the relevant curriculum framework(s) as appropriate to the ages, needs and abilities of the pupils you work with and the requirements of your school. This includes preparing, implementing and monitoring curriculum plans according to the curriculum frameworks for education for your home country: England, Northern Ireland, Scotland or Wales (see above).

Planning learning activities

Effective planning is based on pupils' individual needs, abilities and interests, hence the importance of accurate pupil observations and assessments (see sections on observing and assessing development in Chapter 1 and making assessments in Chapter 14). These needs should be integrated into the learning activities for the pupils you work with. These learning activities must be related to the relevant curriculum requirements applicable to the pupils in your own country and workplace (see above section on curriculum frameworks).

Planning learning activities involves a continuous cycle of: identifying learning needs; preparing, organising and implementing learning activities; observing and recording pupil responses; evaluating learning activities and identifying future learning needs.

The planning process involves:

1. Identification of individual learning needs.
2. Specification of intended learning outcomes for the pupil(s).
3. Preparation for the learning activity.
4. Selection of resources for the learning activity.
5. Organisation of the learning activity.
6. Identification of staff roles.
7. Implementation of the learning activity.
8. Observation and recording of pupil responses including achievements/difficulties.
9. Evaluation of the learning activity.
10. Identification of future learning needs.

You will need to follow the agreed plans for all learning activities. When providing support for learning activities, you may be working with several plans:

- An overall curriculum plan (usually linked to a topic or theme) demonstrating how the teacher intends to extend pupils' learning within the National Curriculum, the National Literacy Strategy and the National Numeracy Strategy Frameworks.
- Lesson or activity plans with detailed information about the learning activities including specific learning objectives, resources/staff required and support strategies.
- A timetable for the school day outlining when and where the learning activities will take place and including routines that have to be done at specific times, e.g. registration, break/playtime, lunchtime, assembly, home time.
- Structured learning programmes for individual pupils, such as particular activities to encourage the development of pupils with special educational needs, including Individual Education Plans and individual Behaviour Support Plans.

The teaching assistant's role in planning learning activities

Advanced planning and the detailed preparation of work are central to the effective delivery of the curriculum and to providing appropriate support for teaching and learning. Teachers should involve teaching assistants in the planning and preparation of their work by having regular planning meetings about once a term or every half term. In addition, each day the teacher and the teaching assistant should discuss:

- the teacher's lesson plans
- the objectives of the learning activities
- the teaching assistant's contribution to learning activities
- the type and level of support for the pupils
- the specific strategies for supporting learning activities.

These regular planning meetings and discussions will help to avoid confusion as both the teacher and the teaching assistant will then be clear about the exact tasks to be performed and the level of support to be provided. Short discussions after lessons are also helpful as teaching assistants can provide feedback to the teacher about the progress of pupils during group or individual learning activities. This feedback can make a valuable contribution to the teacher's assessment of pupils and help with the future planning of learning activities.

As directed by the teacher, you will need to plan, implement and evaluate the learning activities of the pupil or pupils you work with in the school. When planning and/or implementing learning activities, your overall aims should be to:

- support all the pupils you work with as directed by the teacher
- ensure each pupil has full access to the curriculum
- encourage participation by all pupils
- meet pupils' individual learning needs
- build on pupils' existing knowledge and skills
- enable all pupils to achieve their full learning potential.

Some classrooms have a teaching assistant folder that is kept on the teacher's desk or teaching base. The teacher may write notes for the teaching assistant in an exercise book or there may be separate teaching assistant plans for each lesson or learning activity. These teaching assistant plans may include space for you to record what you actually did and what happened to the pupils.

Subject:	Completed by:	Time:	Location:	Duration:
Date:	Class:	Year:	Number:	Term:

Curriculum/strategy links:

Children's previous experiences:

Learning objectives:

Differentiation:	Support needs:
Resources:	Health and safety:
Key Questions:	Key Vocabulary:

Organisation/Content Introduction:	Teaching Assistant Activity:	Pupil Activity:
Organisation/Content Main:	Teaching Assistant Activity:	Pupil Activity:
Organisation/Content Plenary:	Teaching Assistant Activity:	Pupil Activity:

Assessment: Who?	Criteria:	Strategies:	Evidence/recording:
Notes			

Figure 7.6: Planning sheet for teaching assistant

 **Activity!**

Give examples of how you plan activities.

Supporting the teacher in the delivery of learning activities

The teaching assistant supports the delivery of learning activities as directed by the teacher. To provide effective support the teaching assistant must know and understand the objectives of the learning activities and the strategies to support pupils' learning.

As a teaching assistant, you should be aware of your experience and expertise in relation to supporting learning activities and how this relates to the planned activities. You should ensure that you are adequately prepared for your contribution to the learning activities, such as understanding the relevant subject knowledge and support strategies as well as obtaining appropriate resources. This may mean discussing development opportunities to improve your skills in areas where you currently lack experience or expertise (see Chapter 9).

When supporting learning activities you should remember these important points:

1. **Develop an effective partnership with the class teacher:** know and understand your exact role; know and understand the teacher's role; contribute to the planning of learning activities; use the same strategies as the teacher to support learning; share the same goals as the teacher for pupils' learning and establish good communication with the teacher.

2. **Follow agreed class rules and class routines:** how the pupils enter and exit the classroom; classroom organisation; the storage and use of materials and equipment; discipline – approaches to pupil behaviour; rewards and sanctions and marking work.

3. **Understand the teaching methods for learning activities:** class teaching; question time; group work and individual tasks.

4. **Provide effective support during learning activities:** understand requirements of the lesson; know the intended learning outcomes for pupils; prepare and organise resources as directed by the teacher; know the group, e.g. their character, ability, strengths, individual needs, etc; know what support individuals within the group may need; use appropriate support strategies and give the teacher feedback on the pupils' responses including their achievements and any difficulties experienced during the learning activity.

(Balshaw and Farrell, 2002)

The teaching assistant's role in delivering learning activities

Your role will depend on the school and your own experience and/or qualifications. As a teaching assistant you may have a general role working with different classes in a year group/ key stage or specific responsibilities for a pupil, subject area or age group. When working with a specific pupil or pupils you should have information regarding their special educational needs and any special provision including details of statements of special educational needs, Individual Education Plans and/or Behaviour Support Plans. You may be involved in implementing a structured programme designed by a specialist such as a speech and language therapist (see Chapter 12).

When delivering learning activities you should ensure that you make accurate and detailed records of what has been planned and delivered in order to: clarify the aims and learning objectives of activity plans; avoid contradictory strategies/unnecessary duplication of work; use the time available more effectively; evaluate the success of plans/activities and provide continuity and progression for future planning.

Preparing for learning activities

The teacher's short-term plans (e.g. individual lesson plans and/or activity plans) should include information about your role in delivering learning activities. These plans should include the learning objectives and the teacher's expectations of what the learning outcomes for the pupils might be. Use your personal timetable, the class timetable and the available systems of communication within the school to help you know and understand: what you have to do before you deliver the learning activity; where, when and with whom the learning activity will take place and why the learning activity is being implemented.

You need the relevant lesson plans at least the day before so that you have time to prepare what you need for the learning activities. This preparation may involve: finding resources; doing some photocopying; checking equipment and its availability; reading up on a subject; finding artefacts or reference books for the pupils or asking the teacher for further information.

You need time and the opportunity to discuss the teacher's plans beforehand. If you do not understand any aspect of the learning activities you are expected to support, then you must ask the teacher for further information. You will not be able to provide effective support for the pupils unless you are absolutely clear about the requirements of each learning activity (Watkinson, 2003).

Your role in delivering learning activities involves assisting the teacher by:

- preparing the learning environment to meet the individual learning needs of each pupil in the class
- providing appropriate learning activities for individuals and groups of pupils
- selecting and using appropriate learning materials
- supervising an individual or small group of pupils
- maintaining pupil safety during the learning activity
- interacting with the pupils in ways that focus their attention on the learning potential of the learning materials, e.g. asking questions such as 'What happens if you do...?'
- using praise and encouragement to help pupils participate fully in learning activities
- observing pupil responses during the learning activity (see below).

 **Activity!**

Describe your role in delivering learning activities.

Organising learning resources

The learning resources in the school should support learning activities across the full range of the curriculum. A wide variety of learning resources will help to maintain interest in the subject area and help to support individual learning needs. The school should decide on spending priorities when allocating resources as some areas of the curriculum may require more substantial or expensive learning materials than others. Careful criteria should be set for selecting and using learning resources. For example: health and safety; ages/ability levels of the pupils; quality and durability; versatility and value for money; special educational needs

Figure 7.7: Teaching assistant supporting pupils during a learning activity

(e.g. specialist or modified learning materials) and equal opportunities (e.g. resources reflecting positive images of cultural diversity, gender roles and people with disabilities).

The organisation of learning resources is also an important consideration. For example, to encourage independent learning, classroom resources should be organised in ways that allow pupils to locate the learning resources they need and to put them away afterwards. Learning resources should be clearly labelled and stored where they are accessible to the pupils. Learning resources must be regularly maintained, cleaned and checked for damage. Items that are incomplete, unhygienic or past repair should be appropriately discarded.

Figure 7.8: Supporting children's learning

Providing support for learning activities

When supporting learning activities you will need to: deliver learning activities as directed by the teacher; use appropriate resources and support strategies for each pupil's needs and abilities; adapt learning activities to meet the learning objectives; assist each pupil at an appropriate level and promote independent learning (see below).

The strategies to support learning should ensure that each pupil participates fully in every lesson. As a teaching assistant you should:

- Ensure that pupils in your group(s) concentrate and behave responsibly.
- Ensure that pupils understand and follow the teacher's instructions.
- Remind pupils of teaching points made by the teacher.
- Translate or explain words and phrases used by the teacher.
- Use the correct language and vocabulary for the learning activity.
- Question pupils and encourage their participation.
- Organise and participate in appropriate play activities or games.
- Help pupils to use equipment and resources relevant to the learning activity.
- Use visual or practical aids, or a computer with suitable software, especially when supporting pupils with special educational needs.
- Look for and note any common problems that pupils have, or mistakes that they make, so that the teacher can address these in future learning activities.

Promoting independent learning

You need to arrange with the teacher the strategies and resources to be used to promote independent learning. To promote independent learning you can: encourage and support pupils in making decisions about their own learning; provide appropriate levels of assistance for individual pupils; use technology to enable pupils to work more independently; provide challenges to promote independent learning and encourage pupils to review their own learning strategies, achievements and future learning needs. All pupils should be encouraged to develop independent learning in preparation for the next key stage, college, work and adult life.

Younger pupils should be encouraged to develop these independent learning skills:

- take turns to speak and listen
- respond appropriately to other pupils and adults
- know, understand and apply class/school rules
- ask an appropriate adult for help
- make choices about books
- listen carefully and follow verbal instructions
- use pre-selected learning materials for independent learning
- select resources independently
- follow simple written instructions
- work with a partner to check or review work
- use spelling aids, e.g. individual wordbooks, topic word banks and simple dictionaries
- use the school library with support
- access information from pictures, artefacts, simple charts and diagrams with support.

Older pupils should be encouraged to continue using the skills listed above and also to develop these independent learning skills:

- start work independently
- interpret written instructions independently
- work cooperatively with other pupils
- manage own reading book and help keep reading record up-to-date
- put name on any loose paperwork
- put correct date on all work
- aim to complete all tasks set in a given time
- carefully organise and keep own work
- be able to make notes during lessons
- use the school library independently
- use computers independently
- access information from artefacts, simple charts, diagrams and text with increasing independence
- use information from various sources and include references.

Activity!

- What strategies have you used to support pupils' learning?
- Give examples of how you have promoted independent learning, e.g. using ICT skills.

Pupil responses and preferences

Pupil responses should also be considered when providing support for learning activities. Take notice of non-verbal responses and preferences demonstrated by the pupils; these are just as important as what the pupil says. You should be sensitive to pupil needs and desires. Despite careful planning, you may find that when you are delivering a learning activity it is not appropriate for all the pupils you are working with. You will need to monitor pupils' responses to learning activities and take appropriate action to modify or adapt activities to achieve the intended learning objectives or provide additional activities to extend their learning.

You can use pupils' positive or negative responses to modify or extend activities to meet each pupil's needs more effectively. For example, if the learning objectives prove too easy or too difficult, you may have to set new goals. By breaking down learning activities into smaller tasks, you may help individual pupils to achieve success more quickly. You may need to provide an alternative version of the activity or you may be able to present the learning materials in different ways or offer a greater/lesser level of assistance.

You may need to modify or adapt activities for the following reasons: the pupil lacks concentration; the pupil is bored or uninterested; the pupil finds the activity too difficult or too easy or the pupil is upset or unwell (if so, you may need to abandon/postpone the activity). In modifying plans you are continuing a cycle of planning and implementing activities. Remember to give the pupils positive encouragement and feedback to reinforce and sustain their interest and efforts in the learning process. (See section on the importance of praise and encouragement in Chapter 3.)

Dealing with problems and difficulties

Regular observations and evaluations of learning activities are helpful in identifying any potential problems pupils may have in their development, learning or behaviour. By carefully observing pupils during learning activities you can identify: the ways in which individual pupils learn; how pupils interact with each other, e.g. behaviour and social skills and any difficulties pupils may have during the learning activity, e.g. following instructions, performing the necessary skills or understanding concepts.

A continuous record of a pupil's learning difficulties can help identify specific problems. Working with parents, colleagues and specialist advisors (if necessary) the teacher can then plan a suitable programme to enable the pupil to overcome these difficulties. Observations can provide a check that the pupil's learning is progressing in the expected ways. You will need to be able to resolve any difficulties you may have in supporting the learning activities as planned. For example: modifying or adapting an inappropriate activity; coping with insufficient materials or equipment breakdown and dealing with uncooperative or disruptive pupils. You must report any problems you are unable to resolve to the teacher.

Supporting the teacher in the evaluation of learning activities

After you have planned and/or delivered a learning activity, you will need to evaluate it. Some evaluation also occurs during the learning activity, providing continuous assessment of a pupil's performance. It is important to evaluate the learning activity so that you can: identify if the learning activity has been successful, e.g. the aims and learning objectives or outcomes have been met; consider the ways in which the learning activity might be modified/adapted to meet the individual learning needs of the pupil or pupils; provide information on learner responses and whether or not a particular learning activity has been successful to the teacher, SENCO or other professionals.

Evaluating learning activities

When involved in evaluating learning activities for an individual pupil or group of pupils remember these important points:

- How do the pupil or pupils respond to the learning activity?
- Do you need to adapt the original plan, e.g. change the resources or the timing of the learning activity?
- Did the pupil(s) achieve the intended learning objectives?
- How effective was the preparation and delivery of the learning activity?
- Make a note of pupil achievements and/or any difficulties.
- Record these using methods as appropriate to your role.
- Report achievements, difficulties or concerns to the teacher.
- Have you identified any future learning needs for the pupil(s) as a result of pupil responses during this learning activity?
- Are there any possible modifications you could make for future learning activities?
- Discuss your ideas with the teacher.

Providing information on pupil progress and responses

You will need to keep accurate records of pupil progress and responses to learning activities in order to feed back information to the teacher and other relevant people. You can record significant aspects of pupil participation and progress during the learning activity (if possible) or shortly afterwards so that you remember important points.

After the activity, use all the available relevant information to evaluate the effectiveness of your planning and implementation of the activity, e.g. information from parents, colleagues and other professionals. You must provide feedback about the pupils' learning achievements to the teacher. Any suggested changes to future activity plans should be agreed with the teacher and other relevant staff.

You can provide information on pupil progress and responses by considering these questions:

1. Did the pupil(s) achieve the objectives/outcomes set? If not, why not?
2. If the pupil(s) has achieved the objectives, what effect has it had? (e.g. on behaviour, learning or any special need).
3. Were the objectives too easy or too hard for the pupil(s)?
4. How did any staff involvement affect pupil(s) achievement?
5. Was the lesson or activity plan successful? If not, why not?

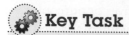 **Key Task**

1. Describe *two* learning activities you have helped to plan, deliver and evaluate. Include information on: a brief description of each learning activity; the objectives of each learning activity; a list of materials and/ or equipment used; your contribution to the learning activities; the type and level of support for the pupils; the specific strategies for supporting learning activities; an evaluation of each learning activity.
2. Include copies of planning and evaluation sheets.

NOS Links:

Level 2:   STL 1.1   STL 1.2   STL 1.3

Summary of key points in this chapter:

- **Understanding pupil development and learning** including: how children think and learn; learning experiences; patterns of learning; active learning; learning styles; factors affecting learning.
- **Curriculum frameworks** including: the Early Years Foundation Stage; The National Curriculum in England; Curriculum frameworks in Northern Ireland, Scotland and Wales.
- **Curriculum plans** including: long-term plans; medium-term plans; short-term plans.
- **Supporting the teacher in the planning of learning activities** including: planning learning activities; the teaching assistant's role in planning learning activities.
- **Supporting the teacher in the delivery of learning activities** including: the teaching assistant's role in delivering learning activities; preparing for learning activities; organising learning resources; providing support for learning activities; promoting independent learning; pupil responses and preferences; dealing with problems and difficulties.
- **Supporting the teacher in the evaluation of learning activities** including: evaluating learning activities; providing information on pupil progress and responses.

Further Reading

Balshaw, M. and Farrell, P. (2002) *Teaching Assistants: Practical Strategies for Effective Classroom Support*. David Fulton Publishers.

Bentham, S. (2003) *A Teaching Assistant's Guide to Child Development and Psychology in the Classroom*. Routledge.

Brookes, G. (2008) *The Complete Guide for Teaching Assistants in Secondary Education*. Continuum International Publishing Group Ltd.

Cheminais, R. (2008) *Every Child Matters: A Practical Guide for Teaching Assistants*. David Fulton Publishers.

Dean, J. (2005) *The Teaching Assistant's Guide to Primary Education*. Routledge Falmer.

Dupree, J. (2005) *Help Students Improve Their Study Skills: A Handbook for Teaching Assistants in Secondary Schools*. David Fulton Publishers Ltd.

Hutchin, V. (2007) *Supporting Every Child's Learning Across the Early Years Foundation Stage*. Hodder Murray.

QCDA (2010) *The National Curriculum: Primary Handbook*. Qualifications and Curriculum Development Agency.
http://curriculum.qcda.gov.uk/uploads/FINAL_-_Handbook_complete_(reprint_version)_tcm8-18066.pdf

8. Supporting positive behaviour

> **This chapter relates to QCF unit:**
>
> TDA 2.9 Support positive behaviour

Expectations for behaviour

Pupil <u>behaviour</u> can be defined as a pupil's actions and reactions or a pupil's treatment of others. Behaviour involves children *learning to conform* to parental expectations for behaviour, school expectations for behaviour and society's expectations for behaviour.

key words

Behaviour: a person's actions, reactions and treatment of others.

Parental expectations for behaviour

Parents have expectations for their children's behaviour based on: the media; cultural or religious beliefs; individual variations in child-rearing practices; adherence to traditional child-rearing practices; comparisons to other children (of relatives, friends and neighbours); perceptions of their own childhood and *their* parents' attitudes to behaviour.

Many parents may have idealised or unrealistic expectations concerning their children's behaviour because some childcare/education books and the media promote unrealistic age-related expectations so that many children do not seem to 'measure up' to what the experts say. Smaller families (often with few or no relatives nearby) mean many parents lack first-hand experience of caring for children *before* they have their own children and may feel less confident about their parenting skills. Parents of children with special needs may be unsure of what to expect from their children in terms of behaviour; they may over compensate for their child's special needs by being over protective or by letting the child get away with behaviour that would not be appropriate in a child of similar age/level of development.

In the past children did not dare challenge parental authority for fear of physical punishment. Today some parents still feel that if they were brought up this way, then this is how they expect their children to behave. In the 21st century, society recognises the rights of the child and has the expectation that all parents should be more caring and responsive to their children's needs by using positive methods such as praise, encouragement, negotiation and rewards to achieve appropriate behaviour. Children learn what their parents consider to be appropriate behaviour and will bring these expectations to the childcare setting. Children also observe their parents' behaviour that may be:

- Assertive: sensitive to their own *and* other people's needs
- Passive: too sensitive to other people's needs so *ignores own needs*
- Aggressive: obsessed with own needs so *ignores other people's needs*.

The school's expectations for pupil behaviour

Children who are not prepared (or are unable) to conform
have to accept the consequences, such as sanctions or
punishments for unacceptable behaviour. Learning about
behaviour (as with all learning) always takes place within a
social context. Certain types of behaviour may be acceptable
in one context but not in another (e.g. families may make

 key words

Social context: *any* situation or
environment where social interaction
occurs, e.g. home, nursery, school,
local community.

allowances for their child's behaviour), however different rules apply in school because
adults must consider the needs of *all* pupils. What is acceptable in one situation may not be
acceptable in another, even within the same school, for example loud, boisterous behaviour
is acceptable in the playground but *not* in the classroom. Conforming brings limitations to
pupils' behaviour, for example following school rules and participating in all curriculum areas
even those they do not like.

 **Activity!**

What are *your* expectations regarding what is acceptable behaviour for yourself, for the
pupils in your school and for the individual in society?

Other influences on pupil behaviour

The media (television, magazines and comics) and computer games can have positive or
negative influences on pupil behaviour, depending on what the children see and how they
are affected by it. Children exposed to violent images may see aggressive behaviour as an
acceptable way to deal with others. Children who observe more assertive behaviour (with
its emphasis on negotiation and compromise) are likely to demonstrate similar positive
behaviour. Television programmes, characters and personalities provide powerful role models
for children's behaviour. Just consider the effectiveness of advertising!

Peer pressure may have a negative influence on pupil behaviour as other children may:
persuade them to participate in dangerous activities including 'dares'; pressure them into
socially unacceptable behaviour, e.g. lying, stealing or bullying; exclude or threaten them if
they do not conform or encourage them to act in ways they never would as an individual, e.g.
'mob rule'. However, you can sometimes use peer pressure to encourage positive behaviour by
highlighting the positive benefits of certain behaviour for the group, class or school.

Providing positive role models

Children model their attitudes and actions on the behaviour of others. They imitate the actions
and speech of those they are closest to, e.g. acting at being 'mum', 'dad', 'nursery nurse', 'play
worker' or 'teacher'; copying the actions and mannerisms of adults around the home, childcare
setting or school. All adults working with children need to be aware of the significant impact
they make to children's social (and emotional) development by providing positive role models.
When working with pupils you should strike a balance between allowing for the children's

increasing need for independence and providing adequate supervision with appropriate guidelines for socially acceptable behaviour. Observing the behaviour of parents and other significant adults (such as childcarers, teachers and teaching assistants) affects children's own behaviour, how children deal with their own feelings and how children relate to others. This is why it is so important for adults to provide positive role models for children's behaviour.

✏ Activity!

- Who were your role models when you were younger? How do you think these early role models influenced your own behaviour?
- How could a teaching assistant model positive behaviour? Give examples from your experiences of working with pupils.

Promoting positive behaviour

Creating an environment that promotes positive behaviour helps to shape the school's ethos and reflect the setting's values. Positive behaviour is an essential building block for creating a welcoming and pleasant learning environment in which all members of the school feel respected, safe and secure. When helping teachers to create an environment that promotes positive behaviour, you should remember that pupils are more likely to behave in positive ways if they are: in a welcoming and stimulating learning environment; engaged in interesting and challenging learning activities that are appropriate to their ages and levels of development; given clear and realistic guidelines on behaviour and work with adults who have positive expectations for pupil behaviour.

Examples of positive pupil behaviour:	Examples of negative pupil behaviour:
Sharing resources and adult's attention; taking turns	Not sharing; attention-seeking; jealousy
Working cooperatively	Disrupting activities, e.g. taking things without asking, fighting or arguing
Being friendly; helping/comforting others	Being aggressive/abusive, e.g. upsetting or hurting others, bullying
Concentrating on activities, e.g. remaining on task	Not concentrating on activities, e.g. being easily frustrated or distracted
Complying with adult requests	Being defiant and refusing reasonable adult requests
Contributing creative ideas	Overriding or ridiculing other people's ideas
Expressing self effectively	Expressing self inappropriately, e.g. emotional outbursts, whining or nagging

Key Task

1. Think about the goals and boundaries that might be appropriate to the pupil or pupils you work with in your school.
2. If possible, encourage the pupil or pupils to draw up their own list of rules that promote positive behaviour.

NOS Links:
Level 2:   STL 3.4   STL 4.1   STL 4.3

Rewards and sanctions

The school behaviour policy should state how the school establishes a climate where praise and encouragement have precedence over the use of sanctions. A wide range of rewards should be available, especially the frequent use of praise during lessons and around the school to show instant recognition for positive behaviour, punctuality and regular attendance. You must know which rewards and sanctions you are free to use and those which you would have to negotiate with, or leave to the teacher, to apply.

Figure 8.4: Using formal rewards

Formal reward systems including credits, merits and prizes can also be used to recognise and congratulate pupils who are good role models for behaviour. Rewards should not be given just to the same 'good' pupils but also to pupils who demonstrate improvement in their own behaviour or attendance (DfES, 2003).

Rewards can provide positive incentives for positive behaviour. Pupils can be motivated by rewards such as: the choice of a favourite activity; special responsibility; smiley faces, stars or stamps; stickers or badges; merit points and certificates; mention in praise assembly; mention in head teacher's praise book or a letter from the head teacher to a pupil's parents.

Rewards are most effective when they are:

- Immediate and clearly linked to the pupil's behaviour, effort or achievement so that the pupil connects the reward with the behaviour.
- Meaningful and appropriate to the pupil's age/level of development, e.g. smiley faces and stickers are more real to younger pupils than merit or house points.
- Related to an individual's behaviour, effort or achievement rather than a group; every pupil needs the chance to obtain rewards for some positive aspect of their own behaviour.
- Recognised and consistently applied by all the staff in the school, e.g. some adults hand out rewards like confetti (making them meaningless), while others strictly ration them (making rewards virtually unobtainable) – either way pupils will not be motivated.

The difficulty with some school reward systems is that pupils who find it easier to behave appropriately may do very well, but those with emotional or behavioural difficulties may not.

Reward systems that display stars or points for the whole group can be particularly damaging to pupils' self-esteem and often they do not indicate what the reward was for. An individual chart or book for each pupil can be better as they are then clearly competing against their own past efforts or improving their own behaviour.

For example, each pupil could have a small exercise book with a page a week for stickers, smiley faces or merit points which are clearly linked to the pupil's behaviour and/or learning. The teacher can negotiate with each pupil the targets they are expected to achieve that particular week. If the pupil achieves this target they receive an appropriate reward such as a certificate or the choice of a favourite activity. This makes it easier for pupils to see their individual efforts and achievements and can also help to set future goals for behaviour and learning.

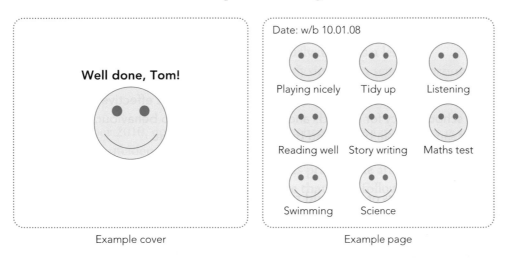

Figure 8.5: Example of individual pupil record of rewards

While the emphasis should be on promoting positive behaviour through encouragement, praise and rewards, there may be times when these do not work. Sometimes it is necessary to impose sanctions for pupils whose behaviour goes beyond acceptable boundaries or who break the school/class/playground rules.

Schools should have a scale of sanctions for inappropriate behaviour. The school behaviour management policy should explain why these sanctions are necessary. Effective sanctions should be designed to discourage inappropriate behaviour rather than to punish pupils who break the rules. Consistency in the application of sanctions is essential and staff should use reprimands sparingly and fairly. Sanctions are more likely to discourage inappropriate behaviour if pupils see them as fair.

The school behaviour management policy should be supported with a range of sanctions for pupils who break the rules, ranging from letters to parents/carers, loss of privileges, detention, right up to exclusion for the most serious or persistent inappropriate behaviour (DfES, 2003).

Sanctions for inappropriate behaviour may include: staff registering disapproval and explaining why to the pupil(s); staff warnings to pupils that their behaviour is unacceptable; 'time out' involving isolation of the pupil for a short period; extra or alternative tasks for the pupil; the pupil losing a privilege, e.g. loss of playtime; the pupil writing a letter of apology or writing about what happened during an incident; the parents being told at the end of the day or a letter

9. Improving own team and practice

This chapter relates to QCF unit:

TDA 2.6 Improve own team and practice

Effective teamwork

When working with others to support teaching and learning in schools, you need to understand your role in contributing to effective teamwork and working effectively with colleagues. Much of adult life involves working with other people, usually in a group or team. Individuals within a team affect each other in various ways. Within the team there will be complex interactions involving different personalities, roles and expectations as well as hidden agendas that may influence the behaviour of individual members of the team. Teamwork is essential when working closely and regularly with other people over a period of time.

Effective teamwork is important because it helps all members of the team to:

- **T**ake effective action when planning and/or assigning agreed work tasks.
- **E**fficiently implement the agreed work tasks.
- **A**gree aims and values which set standards of good practice.
- **M**otivate and support each other.
- **W**elcome feedback about their work.
- **O**ffer additional support in times of stress.
- **R**eflect on and evaluate their own working practices.
- **K**now and use each person's strengths and skills.

Working as part of a team

As a teaching assistant, you need to know and understand the different roles of the team members in your school and the process of decision making within the team. A teaching assistant in a primary, secondary or special school is part of a team which will include some or all of the following: other teaching assistants; class or subject teachers; deputy head teacher; head teacher; special educational needs coordinator (SENCO); specialist teachers, e.g. to support pupils with sensory or physical impairment; parent helpers and/or other volunteers; students on placement from college and pupils on work experience from secondary school.

Activity!

Outline the role and main responsibility of each member of your particular team.

Effective communication with colleagues

You should know how to communicate effectively with members of your team. Effective communication is essential for developing effective team practice. Look back at the list of inter-personal skills needed for effective communication with children (and adults) in Chapter 3. Effective lines of communication are also important to ensure that all members of the team receive the necessary up-to date information to enable them to make a full contribution to the life of the school.

As a teaching assistant you may feel particularly isolated if you work only part time, work in only one class or support an individual pupil with special educational needs. Make sure you check school noticeboards, newsletters and/or staff bulletins for important information. You can also use informal opportunities such as break or lunch times to share information, experiences and ideas with the SENCO, teachers or other teaching assistants. Regular lines of communication are particularly important if more than one teaching assistant works with the same pupil or pupils. You might find a communications book or file useful as well as regular meetings with other teaching assistants. If you are a new (or student) teaching assistant you may benefit from the knowledge and understanding of existing teaching assistants; if you are an experienced teaching assistant you can make a valuable contribution to the induction or ongoing training of new teaching assistants, possibly acting as a mentor.

Participating in team meetings

As a teaching assistant you will also be involved in regular team meetings with the teacher (or teachers) in whose class you work and/or the SENCO. These meetings will enable you to make relevant contributions to provide more effective support for both the teacher and pupils. You may discuss specific plans the teacher has made relating to the pupils' learning, the progress made by pupils, including their achievements and any difficulties, plus the appropriate resources and support approaches.

You may also be invited to more general staff meetings. Where there are logistical problems in all teaching assistants being able to attend all staff meetings, you may be welcome to attend any meeting but be specifically invited to attend meetings where issues are to be discussed that are directly relevant to *your* work in school.

You need to prepare for meetings carefully especially if you have been asked to provide information, for example, on the progress of a pupil with whom you work. Even if you are not required to make a specific contribution you still need to look at the meeting agenda and any relevant reports in advance so that you can participate in discussions during the meeting. At team meetings, participate in ways which are consistent with your role as a teaching assistant. Ensure your contributions are relevant and helpful to the work of the team. Express your opinions in a clear, concise manner and demonstrate respect for the contributions made by other team members. Make notes during the meeting to remind yourself of any action *you* need to take as a result of the issues discussed and decisions made by the team.

Summary of key points in this chapter:

- **The provision of ICT equipment in school** including: the range of ICT equipment; the location of ICT equipment; following operating procedures and safety requirements.
- **The school policy for use of ICT in school** including: virus controls and other measures to protect pupils; data protection and ICT; child protection and ICT.
- **Supporting the development of ICT skills in pupils** including: ICT skills in primary schools; ICT skills in secondary schools; the teaching assistant's role in supporting the development of ICT skills; promoting independence in the use of ICT.
- **Safety and security relating to ICT equipment** including: ways to minimise risks when using ICT equipment; storage and security of ICT equipment.

Further Reading

Galloway, J. (2004) *ICT for Teaching Assistants.* David Fulton Publishers.

Galloway, J. (2006) *Primary ICT for Teaching Assistants.* David Fulton Publishers.

Siraj-Blatchford, J. and Whitebread, D. (2003) *Supporting ICT in the Early Years.* Open University Press.

Stansfield, J. (ed) (2004) *A First Handbook of ICT and Special Educational Needs.* NASEN Enterprises Ltd.

Williams, G. (2007) *ICT Explained: A Guide for Support Staff.* 4th edition. Pearson Publishing.

11. Supporting learning environments

This chapter relates to QCF units:

TDA 2.11 Contribute to supporting bilingual learners

TDA 2.12 Prepare and maintain learning environments

TDA 2.13 Provide displays in schools

TDA 2.16 Support children and young people's play and leisure

Helping to organise the learning environment

Central to creating an appropriate learning environment for all pupils in school is providing space, time and resources relevant to the needs of the pupils and the requirements of the curriculum for your home country. As well as provision for the curriculum subjects, there should be regular times for routines such as playtimes/breaks, lunchtime, lunchtime clubs and after school activities. A daily routine provides stability and security for pupils. The class timetable should be clearly displayed in a manner appropriate to the ages of the pupils; older pupils should have their own copy of their weekly timetable. Flexibility is also important to allow for special events such as educational visits, swimming lessons or visitors to the school.

The precise way the learning environment is organised depends on: specific curriculum requirements; the resources for particular subject areas; the learning objectives for the pupils; individual teaching and learning styles; behaviour management strategies and the inclusion of pupils with special educational needs. Effective organisation is also influenced by the general quality of the learning environment. The learning environment should have:

- **Adequate floor space for the age, size and needs of the pupils.** This means teaching space including space for teaching assistants to work with individuals or groups of pupils as needed. Pupils with physical disabilities may require additional floor space for wheelchairs and other specialised equipment or furniture. Pupils with emotional and/or behavioural difficulties may also benefit from adequate personal classroom space.
- **Appropriate sources of heating, lighting and ventilation.** Pupils need to work in an environment that is neither too hot nor too cold as these can affect concentration levels. The heating source must be safe and fitted/maintained to the required legal standards. There should be good sources of both natural and artificial light.

- **Appropriate acoustic conditions** to enable pupils to listen during essential discussions and to help reduce noise levels. Carpeted floor areas, sound absorbent screens, displays, drapes and curtains all help to absorb reverberation.
- **Adequate storage space** for the materials and equipment needed to meet the demands of the National Curriculum. There should also be space for computer workstations with access to mains power.

The classroom layout should be free from clutter and easily accessible to all pupils, including those with physical disabilities or sensory impairment. The learning environment should also be welcoming and user-friendly. This includes taking account of cultural differences by providing displays and notices which reflect the cultural diversity of the school and local community.

 Key Task

With the class teacher's permission, take a photograph of the classroom and comment on how the learning environment provides:

- adequate floor space for the age, size and needs of the children
- appropriate sources of heating, lighting and ventilation
- appropriate acoustic conditions
- adequate storage space for materials and equipment
- access for all pupils including those with physical disabilities or sensory impairment.

NOS Links:

Level 2:   STL 1.1   STL 2.4   STL 3.1

As part of your role of assisting the teacher with the organisation of the learning environment, you may be responsible for:

- A group of pupils, and be involved in setting out materials or helping the pupils to access them, explaining a task, maintaining their concentration and interest, asking and/or answering questions, helping pupils to clear away afterwards before moving on to support them with their next activity.
- A specific activity with different groups of pupils throughout the day or week (e.g. supporting literacy, numeracy, science or ICT).
- A pupil with special educational needs, and ensuring that they have the necessary materials and equipment to participate in the lesson including any specialist equipment.

In addition to knowing the timetable for the pupil and/or class you work with, you should have your own timetable showing where, what and with whom you are working throughout the school day. (Detailed information about your roles and responsibilities can be found in Chapter 5.)

 **Activity!**

- Outline the daily/weekly routine for the pupil and/or class whose learning you support.
- Provide a copy of your own personal timetable.

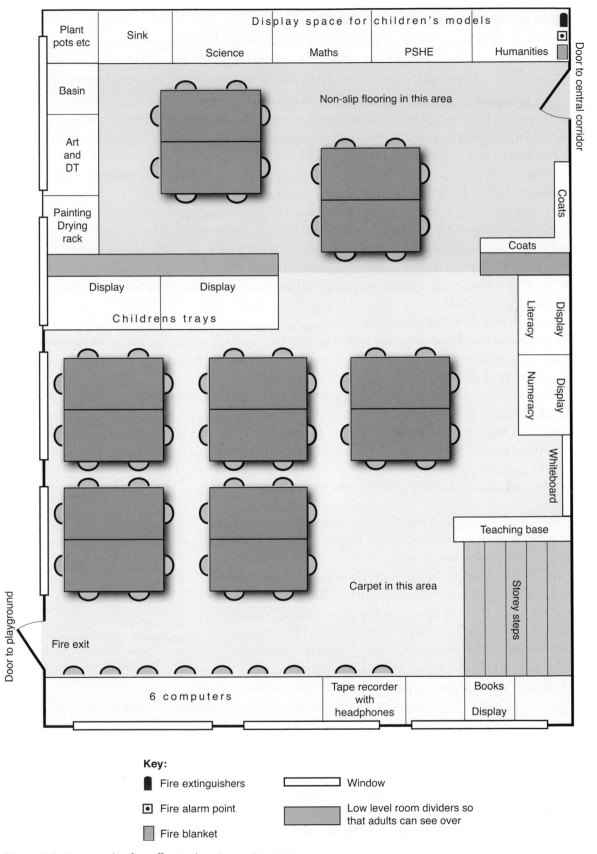

Figure 11.1: An example of an effective learning environment

Organising classroom resources

Every classroom is equipped with a basic set of resources and books appropriate to the age range. Care is taken to ensure that resources reflect the cultural and linguistic diversity of our society, and that all pupils have equality of access. Examples of general classroom resources include:

- Visual aids: wall displays including pupils' work, maps, pictures and posters; interest tables with interesting objects related to topic work; 3D displays of pupils' work including construction models; videos; computer graphics and books. Displays in the classroom reflect the linguistic and cultural diversity of the school.
- Groups of tables for whole class and group work including literacy and numeracy activities.
- Groups of tables for 'messy' practical activities (e.g. art and design, design technology) including storage for art/design materials and equipment, e.g. paint, paint pots, drying rack; sink for washing paint pots and brushes and basin for washing hands.
- Some computers and a printer with selection of appropriate software (see below).
- Tape recorder/compact disc player with headphones with a selection of audiotapes/CDs.
- Book/story corner with appropriate range of fiction and non-fiction books including some dual language books.
- Storage units for specific curriculum areas.
- White board, over-head projector and teaching base including marker pens, transparencies, textbooks, teaching manuals and other resources needed by the teacher or teaching assistant on a regular basis.
- Writing and drawing materials including a variety of writing tools (crayons, pencils, pens, pastels, chalks); different shapes, sizes and types of paper (e.g. plain, coloured, graph).
- Children's work trays to store individual exercise books for literacy, numeracy and science; individual folders for topic work; individual reading books and reading logs; personal named pencils and individual crayon tins.
- Area with individual coat pegs for coats and PE bags.

The learning environment will also have specialist resources to support specific curriculum areas: English; Mathematics; Science; Information and Communication Technology (ICT); Art and Design; Design Technology; Food Technology; Physical Education (PE); Music; PSHE, Citizenship, Religious Studies, Geography and History. Specialist resources include: videos, maps, posters, pictures, artefacts, and story and information books related to class topics or themes. Specialist resources should be stored in the appropriate curriculum resource cupboard or area, and be regularly audited by the curriculum subject coordinator. Staff may contact curriculum subject co-ordinators with suggestions for specialist materials that may need ordering. If you support pupils' learning in any of these areas then you need to be aware of the specific resources and any particular safety requirements.

 key words

General classroom resources: equipment and materials that support all areas of the curriculum, e.g. pictures, posters and 3D displays, books, computers, white board, writing and drawing materials.

Specialist resources: to support specific curriculum areas, e.g. mathematical and scientific equipment, art and design materials, maps, books and DVDs relating to specific subjects.

Activity!

- What are general classroom resources?
- What are specialist resources for specific curriculum areas? If possible, give examples from the resources you use on a regular basis.

Here are some general guidelines about organising resources and materials in the classroom:

- Fire exits must not be obstructed, locked or hidden from view.
- Chairs and tables need to be the correct size and height for the age and level of development of the children.
- Books, jigsaws, art/design materials and computers need to be used in areas with a good source of light, if possible near a source of natural light.
- Water, sand, Art and Design Technology activities need to be provided in an area with an appropriate floor surface with washing facilities nearby.
- Ensure that activities requiring maximum concentration such as literacy or numeracy activities are not on the direct route to the hand-washing area or too close to messy/noisy activities or doorways.
- Any large or heavy equipment that has to be moved for use should be close to where it is stored.

Checking classroom resources

As part of your role you may need to make regular checks to ensure that essential materials or equipment are not running out. Clearing away equipment and materials provides you with a regular opportunity to check whether classroom supplies are running low. You may need to keep a weekly check on **consumable resources** such as art and craft materials, paper, cardboard and other stationery items. Items such as soap, paper towels and so on may need to be checked everyday. When the class teacher or teaching assistant requires resources, a stock requisition form should be completed and given to the person responsible for the storage area. **Non-consumable resources** are things like teaching packs, flashcards, posters and books. When you need to borrow non-consumable resources, it is necessary to sign them out. There should be a logbook in each storage area for this purpose. There will be an inventory or stock list for classroom resources that is checked on a regular basis. Larger items such as classroom furniture may be included on an inventory that is checked annually. There will be a school procedure for doing this.

 key words

Consumable resources: materials that get used up such as stationery items (e.g. paper, cardboard, glue, pens, pencils, exercise books), cleaning materials and ingredients for cooking activities.

Non-consumable resources: equipment and materials that do not get used up such as furniture, computers, books, teaching packs, posters and play equipment.

 Key Task

- Outline your main role and responsibilities for helping to organise the learning environment?
- What are the school's procedures for monitoring and maintaining the supply of classroom resources?
- What are your role and responsibility in relation to these procedures? Include examples of different records you have used to monitor and maintain the supply of classroom resources, e.g. copies of stock requisition form, inventory or stock list.

NOS Links:

Level 2:   STL 1.1   STL 2.4   STL 3.1

Bury College
Woodbury LRC

Encouraging pupils to help maintain their learning environment

The routine of getting out and putting away equipment is part of the learning experience for pupils. This routine helps younger pupils to develop mathematical concepts such as sorting and matching sets of objects and judging space, capacity and volume. It helps all pupils to develop a sense of responsibility for caring for their own learning environment. Pupils of all ages can also gain confidence and independence when involved in setting out and clearing away learning materials as appropriate to their age/level of development and any safety requirements. Materials and equipment should be stored and/or displayed in ways that will enable pupils to choose, use and return them easily. You must ensure that pupils only help in ways that are in line with the school's health and safety policy. Pupils must never have access to dangerous materials such as bleach or use very hot water for cleaning and they should not carry large, heavy or awkward objects due to the potential risks of serious injury. (Detailed information about health and safety is in Chapter 6.)

Providing displays

Part of your role may involve providing visual and tactile displays to support learning environments by stimulating the curiosity and involvement of pupils. When providing displays you need to consider these important points:

1. The purpose of the display, e.g. to stimulate discussion and to consolidate learning.
2. The choice of materials, e.g. the colour and texture of backing paper; using drapes or boxes to create 3D effects; different ways to frame/mount 2D work to make it more eye-catching.
3. The vocabulary and size of lettering, e.g. use words and lettering appropriate to the children's ages and levels of development; remember to use the school's preferred handwriting style or word process captions using an appropriate font.
4. Use appropriate equipment, e.g. paper trimmers, scissors, glue and staple gun.

You should display the work of pupils in ways that encourage creativity and positive self-esteem. Focus on the creative process of children's pictures and writing not the end product. Give children lots of praise for their attempts at creating pictures, models or written work and put their efforts on display. Do not worry that the finished results do not look neat, especially in the early years; it is having a go that is important. Where appropriate encourage the pupils to use their ICT skills to word process their written work and/or to create captions for their pictures and models.

Displays should be appropriate to the work of the learning environment and the children's play and learning needs. Ensure that displays are updated or renewed on a regular basis. Displays in the setting should reflect the linguistic and cultural diversity of the setting and local community. The displays should reflect positive images of race, culture, gender and disability.

Figure 11.2: Interactive display in a classroom

Examples of displays include:

- **Wall displays** to provide a stimulus for discussions and to consolidate learning, including diagrams, maps, posters, pictures and children's work with appropriate labels or captions; alphabet and key words lists; number line and 100 square.
- **Tabletop displays** to stimulate discussion and further learning, including interest tables with interesting artefacts to talk about, look at and explore linked to topics and themes such as colour, shape, sound, musical instruments and texture.
- **Displays of models** made by the children with captions in the form of questions to stimulate discussion, e.g. 'How many...?', 'What will happen if...?'
- **Book displays** to promote children's interest in books, to develop their literacy skills and to extend learning including books relating to topics and themes.

Your tutor/assessor should be able to give you guidance and practical tips on what to do when providing displays. You can also develop your display skills by looking at other people's displays (e.g. senior colleagues) and books about displays (see Further Reading).

 Key Task

Plan, organise and evaluate a display suitable for the pupils you work with. Include the following information:

- the type of display and how it supports learning
- pupil contributions to the display (e.g. drawings, paintings, written work)
- how you made the display
- the effectiveness of the finished display and any possible improvements
- pupil and staff responses to the display
- how the display promotes positive images.

Include a photograph of the finished display.

NOS Links:

Level 2:   **STL 1.1**   **STL 2.4**   **STL 3.1**   **STL 16.1**   **STL 16.2**

Supporting bilingual pupils

Bilingual means 'speaking two languages' which applies to some pupils (and staff) in schools in the United Kingdom. 'Multilingual' is used to describe someone who uses more than two languages. The term 'bilingual' is widely used for all pupils who speak two or more languages.

Promoting language diversity

We live in a multicultural society where a huge variety of languages are used to communicate. We are surrounded by different accents, dialects and other ways of communicating such as sign language. All pupils should have an awareness and understanding of other people's languages, while still feeling proud of their own community language and being able to share this with others. Pupils in schools where only English (or Welsh) is spoken still need an awareness of other languages to appreciate fully the multicultural society they live in.

You must respect the languages of *all* the pupils in your school by working with the teacher to provide an environment which promotes language diversity through: welcoming signs in community languages; learning essential greetings in these languages; displaying photographs and pictures reflecting multicultural images; using labels with different languages/writing styles; sharing books, stories and songs in other languages; providing multicultural equipment, e.g. ethnic dolls, dressing-up clothes, cooking utensils; celebrating festivals and preparing and sharing food from different cultures.

While promoting language diversity we need to remember that we live in a society where English is the dominant language; developing language and literacy skills in English is essential to all pupils if they are to become effective communicators both in and outside the school. Most children starting nursery or school will speak English even if they have a different cultural background. However, there are some children who do start nursery or school with little or no English because they are new to this country or English is not used much at home.

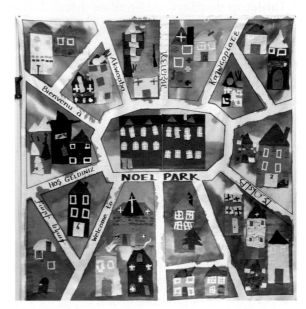

Figure 11.3: Promoting language diversity

 Key Task

- Give examples of how your school promotes language diversity and encourages pupils to use their community languages.
- How do (or could) you provide support for the communication skills of bilingual pupils?

NOS Links:

Level 2:   **STL 2.3**   **STL 4.3**   **STL 6.1**   **STL 10.1**   **STL 11.1**   **STL 11.2**

Supporting pupils with English as an additional language

Since the introduction of the National Literacy Strategy, the preferred term for bilingual pupils is *pupils with English as an additional language* (EAL). There is a broad range of pupils with EAL including pupils who are: literate in English and do not require extra provision; able to converse in English but need help to use language in their school work; literate in languages other than English but need a little extra support with literacy; learning to speak English as well as learning to read and write it or below the levels of language or literacy expected for their age and require adapted materials to meet their language and/or literacy needs.

There are four important factors to consider when providing support for pupils with EAL:

1. **There are different and changing levels of competence involved in speaking two or more languages.** For example, some pupils are still learning their first language while adding words to their second language. Very young children often do 'language

'mixing' which involves combining words from two or more languages when involved in conversations or discussions.

2. **Different situations prompt the use of one language over another.** Pupils who are more fluent in English often use whichever language is appropriate to a particular situation. For example: they might speak to one grandparent using Standard English; speak to another grandparent using Mirpuri and Punjabi; conversations with parents and siblings might involve a mixture of Punjabi and English; and language at the setting might involve the use of a local dialect such as that used in the 'Black Country' in the West Midlands.

3. **The range of communication and literacy skills may be different in each language.** Pupils may be aware of different writing systems being used by their families and in the local community. They may be able to speak a particular language and not be able to write in that language. Pupils may have seen writing which went from right to left as in the Arabic or Hebrew scripts not just from left to right as with English; or they may be used to vertical rather than horizontal writing systems such as Mandarin Chinese or Japanese. Developing literacy skills can be a confusing experience for some pupils with EAL who could be learning to read and write in English in school while learning the same skills in Punjabi at home or in a community school *and* also learning Arabic when studying the Koran at Saturday school.

4. **Changing circumstances can affect a pupil's use of their community language.** For example, moving to a different area where cultural attitudes may be different so that more or less of the pupil's community language is used.

(Whitehead, 1996)

Pupils with English as an additional language do not see their use of different languages as a difficulty. Adults working in schools need to maintain this attitude and to encourage bilingual pupils to see their linguistic abilities as the *asset* it really is in our multicultural society.

You can support pupils with English as an additional language by:

- Encouraging the pupils to use their community languages some of the time; this promotes security and social acceptance which will make learning English easier.
- Asking the teacher to invite parents/grandparents to read or tell stories in community languages or to be involved with small groups for cooking, sewing or craft activities.
- Using songs and rhymes to help introduce new vocabulary.
- Using other areas of the curriculum to develop language skills in a meaningful context, e.g. focus on words used when working on the computer or during science experiments.
- Using play activities and/or games to encourage and extend language.

As well as communication, language and literacy activities you can use other areas of the curriculum to develop language skills in a meaningful context, e.g. use play activities and/or games to encourage and extend language or focus on words used when working on the computer or during science experiments.

Whole-class sessions can provide helpful adult models of spoken English and opportunities for careful listening, oral exchange and supportive, shared repetition. Group work provides opportunities for intensive, focused teaching input. You may need to repeat instructions for pupils with English as an additional language (EAL) and to speak more clearly, emphasising key words, particularly when you are describing tasks that they are to do independently. Encourage them to join in things that all pupils do in chorus: counting, reading aloud whole number sentences, chanting, finger games, songs about numbers and so on. The structure of rhymes and the natural rhythm in songs or poems play an important part in developing number sense in any culture. Use stories and rhymes from a range of cultural backgrounds.

Specialist language support staff can help to ensure that EAL learners are encouraged to apply what they have learnt in the literacy hour across the curriculum. Language support teachers should work with teachers and other staff (e.g. nursery nurses, teaching assistants) to select resources and texts that meet the needs of EAL learners.

It is important to distinguish between pupils who have additional language learning needs and those who also have special educational needs (SEN). Some pupils with EAL may also be assessed as having special educational needs.

Figure 11.4: Teaching assistant supporting a bilingual pupil

(See section on identification, assessment and provision for pupils with SEN in Chapter 12.)

 Key Task

Design and make a booklet about supporting the learning and development of pupils in bilingual or multilingual settings. Include information on the following: the community languages used by the pupils in your school; the school's activities and resources available to support pupils with EAL, e.g. dual language books, bilingual story sessions, language support staff, multilingual resources from the community centre or local education development centre, etc.

NOS Links:

Level 2:   **STL2.3**   **STL4.3**   **STL6.1**   **STL10.1**   **STL11.1**   **STL11.2**

Supporting play and leisure

Play is an essential part of children and young people's development and learning. It is the central way in which children explore and develop an understanding of their environment. Children learn through play. The term 'play' is often used to refer to children's activities that are considered unimportant and frivolous by many people, especially parents. It is up to adults working with children to stress the importance of play to those who are sceptical about its benefits.

Play can help children's development and learning by providing opportunities for:

- self-chosen and well-motivated learning
- challenging and interesting experiences
- taking responsibility for their own learning
- gaining confidence and independence
- cooperative work between children
- developing a wide range of physical skills
- developing problem-solving skills
- encouraging imagination and creativity.

The role of play in children's learning and development

Early learning involves learning through stimulating play activities with appropriate adult support to provide young children with the essential foundations for later learning. Young children who are pushed too hard by being forced to do formal learning activities before they are ready may actually be harmed in terms of their development and they may also be put off literacy, numeracy and other related activities. Young children need a combination of real and imaginary experiences to encourage early learning. This is why play is an important aspect of young children's development and learning. Young children need to handle objects and materials to understand basic concepts. For example, in mathematics using objects for counting and addition such as buttons, cones and plastic cubes. Once children have plenty of practical experiences they can cope more easily with abstract concepts such as written sums or mental arithmetic. Children use play opportunities to encourage and extend the problem-solving abilities that are essential to developing their intellectual processes.

Play activities provide informal opportunities for children to develop ideas and to understand concepts through active learning and communication. Language is a key component in children's thinking and learning. Play is an invaluable way to provide opportunities for language and to make learning more meaningful, especially for young children. Play enables children to learn about concepts in a safe and non-threatening environment. Play activities help to promote all aspects of young children's development.

Social play

Children go through a recognised sequence of social play. Younger children tend to engage in more solitary or parallel play activities because they are more egocentric; while older children are capable of more cooperative play activities as they can take turns, share play equipment and follow rules more easily. There will be times when quite young children can be engaged happily in play activities with some interaction with other children (associative play) such as dressing-up, home corner, doing jigsaws, simple construction or painting. There will be occasions when older children become engrossed in solitary or parallel play activities with no interaction with other children, e.g. doing detailed drawings and paintings, or building intricate constructions that require complete concentration to the exclusion of everyone else.

The sequence of social play

- Solitary play: playing alone.
- Parallel play: playing alongside other children without interaction.
- Associative play: playing alongside other children with limited interaction.
- Cooperative play: playing together.
- Complex cooperative play: playing together including following agreed rules.

A child's level of social interaction during play activities depends on: the individual child; the child's previous experiences of play; the play activity itself and the social context, e.g. the setting and other people present.

Five ways to promote children's learning and development through play

You can help to promote children and young people's learning and development through play by working with others to do the following:

1. Provide challenging and interesting play opportunities appropriate to the ages, needs, interests and abilities of the children and/or young people.

2. Provide a wide range of play opportunities which will help the different aspects of development, e.g. social, physical, intellectual, communication and emotional.

3. Provide varied play resources and encourage children/young people to use them.

4. Participate (where appropriate) in the play activities to stimulate language, extend learning and encourage children and young people's imagination and creative ideas.

5. Encourage social interaction during play, e.g. children may need coaxing to join in or guidance on taking turns and sharing.

Providing for a range of play types

You should know and understand how to provide opportunities for a wide range of play types. Play types can be grouped into three main areas of play – physical, exploratory and imaginative.

Main area of play	Types of play	Example activities
Physical Play activities that provide opportunities for children to develop their physical skills such as gross motor skills, fine motor skills and coordination.	Locomotor play – play involving movement in all directions for its own sake. Mastery play – play involving control of physical aspects of the environment. Rough and tumble play – play involving discovering physical flexibility and demonstrating physical skills.	<ul><li>playing chase, tag, hide and seek</li><li>digging holes, building dens</li><li>play fighting, chasing</li></ul>

Exploratory	Exploratory play – play	• playing with bricks, sand,
Play activities that provide opportunities for children to understand the world around them by exploring their environment and experimenting with materials.	involving manipulating objects or materials to discover their properties and possibilities. Creative play – play allowing new responses, transformation of information, awareness of connections, with an element of surprise. Objective play – play involving hand–eye co-ordination to manipulate objects in an infinite variety of ways.	water, clay, play-dough) • enjoying creative activities, arts and crafts, using a variety of materials and tools) • examining novel uses for a paintbrush, brick)
Imaginative	Communication play –	• telling jokes, play acting,
Play activities that provide opportunities for children to express feelings and to develop social skills.	play using words, nuances or gestures. Deep play – play allowing risky experiences, to develop survival skills and conquer fears. Dramatic play – play dramatising events in which child is indirect participator. Fantasy play – play rearranging the world in a manner unlikely to occur in real life. Imaginative play – play where conventional rules of the real world not applicable. Social play – play involving social interaction that requires following certain rules or protocols. Socio-dramatic play – play involving enacting intense real life personal or interpersonal experiences. Symbolic play – play allowing controlled, gradual exploration and increased understanding, without risk. Role-play – play exploring human activities on basic level.	singing, storytelling • balancing on a high beam, performing skateboarding stunts • presenting a television show, religious or festive celebrations • playing at being an astronaut or king/queen • pretending to be dog or a superhero • games with rules, conversations • playing house, shops, hospital, dentist • using piece of wood to symbolise a person • doing simple domestic chores, i.e. sweeping with a broom, making telephone calls, driving a car, with or without play equipment

(NPFA et al, 2000)

 **Key Task**

- Give examples of play activities for each play type. Where possible, use examples based on your experiences of helping to provide play opportunities for children and/or young people.
- Explain how each activity could encourage learning and development.

NOS Links:

Level: **STL 10.1**   **STL 10.2**   **STL 10.3**   **STL 10.4**   **STL 10.5**   **STL 15.2**

Identifying play needs and preferences

Play is not an extra – something to be done to keep children quiet or occupied while adults are busy or a reward for children when other tasks have been done. Play is an essential part of children's (and young people's) development and learning. Children's play needs to include opportunities to:

- access safe play spaces
- engage in a wide range of play activities and use a variety of play resources
- learn about and understand the physical world
- develop individual skills and personal resources
- communicate and cooperate with others
- develop empathy for others
- make sense of the world in relation to themselves
- do their own learning, in their own time and in their own way.

You should be able to identify children's play needs and preferences. Play needs are the individual needs of children for play. Preferences are children's choices with regard to play. You can help to identify children's play needs and preferences by observing children playing; interacting with children during play and by consulting children about their play needs and preferences by talking with them and asking for their suggestions about play spaces and resources.

 **Activity!**

- Collect information on the play needs and preferences of the children and/or young people in your setting. Use this information to make suggestions for possible play and leisure activities.
- You could present this information in a booklet or information pack on children's play for parent helpers, volunteers and students.

Planning and preparing play spaces

In order to plan and prepare play spaces it is essential for you to know about the range of different types of play spaces that support and enrich the potential for children's play. <u>Play spaces</u> are areas that support and enrich the potential for children to play (SkillsActive, 2004).

 key words

Play spaces: areas that support and enrich the potential for children and/or young people to play.

Types of play spaces include:

- Care and education settings, run by professional staff such as childcarers, play workers and teaching assistants providing play opportunities, e.g. private and local authority day nurseries, out-of-school clubs providing extra-curricular activities, extended schools.
- 'Formal' play provision run by professional play staff and parent helpers/volunteers, e.g. playgroups, holiday play schemes.
- 'Open access' play facilities operated by professional play workers but where children and young people come and go as they please, e.g. adventure playgrounds, some holiday play schemes, and play buses.
- 'Informal' play facilities that are not staffed, e.g. public parks, play areas and playgrounds, skate parks, basketball courts, football pitches and playing fields.
- Non-designated play spaces used by children and young people especially when there are no other play spaces available, e.g. local streets, outside shops, abandoned buildings, open spaces.

(DCMS, 2004)

Figure 11.5: Children in a school holiday play scheme

 **Activity!**

- What play spaces are provided by your setting?
- Find out about the existing play spaces available in your local area.
- What additional play spaces and resources do you think should be made available to meet the play needs and preferences of the children in your local area?

Planning and creating play spaces

You should aim to provide minimum intervention in play activities while keeping children and young people safe from harm. You should help to create a play environment that will stimulate self-directed play and provide maximum opportunities for children and/or young people to experience a wide variety of play types. You can enrich their play experiences in the following ways: planning and creating play spaces that meet their play needs and preferences; obtaining and/or creating resources for a range of play spaces; fostering positive attitudes; providing new materials and tools to stimulate their exploration and learning and participating in their play if and when invited.

You should use information on play needs and preferences to plan appropriate play opportunities. You can write down your plans for play opportunities on a planning sheet or in an activity file. Your plans may be brief or detailed depending on the requirements of your setting. Some activities may require more detailed preparation and organisation than others, e.g. arts and crafts, cooking, outings, etc.

A plan for a play activity could include the following:

Title: A brief description of the activity.

1. **When?** Date and time of the activity.
2. **Where?** Where the activity will take place, e.g. indoor play area, outdoor play area, local park or playground.
3. **Why?** Outline why you have selected this particular activity, e.g. identified children's play needs and preferences through research, observation or consultation.
4. **What?** What you need to prepare in advance, e.g. selecting or making appropriate resources; buying ingredients, materials or equipment.
5. **How?** How you will organise the activity. Consider any safety requirements. Think about tidying up after the activity, e.g. encouraging the children to help tidy up.

Evaluate the activity afterwards, e.g. the children's response to the activity, the skills and/or learning demonstrated by the children, the effectiveness of your preparation, organisation and implementation. Make a note of your evaluation on the planning sheet or in the activity file. These notes will prove helpful when planning future play opportunities and for providing information to colleagues at regular meetings. (There is more about planning activities in Chapters 1 and 7.)

 **Activity!**

Describe the planning and provision of play opportunities in your setting.

Seven ways to support children and young people's play

Working with others you can provide appropriate types of support for children and young people's play in the following ways:

1. Plan play spaces based on children's play needs and preferences, e.g. find out about children's play and development, observe children's play activities.
2. Involve children in the creation of play spaces, e.g. consult them about the play opportunities and play resources they would like in the setting.
3. Create play spaces that children can adapt to their own needs, e.g. flexible play areas to allow children to spread out during their play.
4. Allow children to choose and explore play spaces for themselves, e.g. selecting their own play activities and play resources.

5. Allow children to develop through play in their own ways, e.g. freedom to explore and enjoy their chosen play activities in their own way and in their own time.

6. Allow children's play to continue uninterrupted, e.g. participate in their play as and when invited to do so; only intervene in children's play in order to maintain their physical safety or emotional security.

7. Address the possible barriers to accessing play spaces that some children may experience, e.g. ensure the play setting is inclusive and encourages participation by all the children including those from ethnic minority backgrounds and those with disabilities.

 **Activity!**

Give examples of how you have supported children and/or young people's play and leisure.

Help children and young people to manage risk during play

When working with children and/or young people, you should help them to manage risk during play as appropriate to their ages and levels of development. Children need opportunities to explore and experiment through play and to try out new, exciting play activities. Many play activities have risks, especially physical activities such as climbing, exploring and swimming. *'Risky activity, and risk taking itself, is recognised as an essential part of growing up.'* (CAPT, 2002) Always follow the relevant setting policies and procedures, e.g. health and safety policy; risk assessment and risk management procedures (see Chapter 2).

Figure 11.6: Adult supporting children's play

 **Activity!**

- Outline your setting's policies and procedures that are relevant to managing risk during play and leisure activities, e.g. health and safety policy; risk assessment and risk management procedures.
- List examples of how you help children to manage risk during play according to these policies and procedures and the ages/levels of development of the children you work with.

Ending play sessions

You should be able to end each play session in a way that is appropriate to the ages/levels of development of the children and young people and the requirements of the setting. For example, warn the children in advance that the play session is coming to an end so that they can finish off what they are doing. Young children especially dislike having their play activities suddenly stopped so giving them a five/ten minute warning can help to avoid emotional outbursts.

Ensure that the play area is clean and tidy at the end of the play session. Encourage the children to tidy up and put away play resources as appropriate to their ages and levels of development. Remember to follow the setting's procedures for tidying up and putting away resources. Let the children have a chance to review their play activities as individuals or in groups, e.g. 'circle time' is and excellent way to finish a play session. Make a note of the children's views as these may form the basis for planning future play sessions.

Follow the setting's procedures for ensuring the safety of the children and young people when leaving the setting, e.g. young children must be collected by a known adult (see section on security arrangements for pupil arrival and departure in Chapter 6). After the children have gone complete any required records (see section on record keeping in Chapter 14).

 Key Task

Describe how you have ended a play session.

NOS Links:

Level 2:   STL 15.4

Summary of key points in this chapter:

- **Helping to organise the learning environment** including: adequate floor space for the age, size and needs of the pupils; appropriate sources of heating, lighting and ventilation; appropriate acoustic conditions; adequate storage space; organising classroom resources; checking classroom resources; encouraging pupils to help maintain their learning environment.
- **Providing displays** including: the purpose of the displays; the choice of materials; using appropriate vocabulary and lettering; using appropriate equipment; involving pupils in creating displays; promoting positive images of race, culture, gender and disability.

- **Supporting bilingual pupils** including: promoting language diversity; supporting pupils with English as an additional language.
- **Supporting play and leisure** including: the role of play in children's learning and development; social play; ways to promote learning and development through play; identifying play needs and preferences; providing for a range of play types; planning and preparing play spaces; obtaining resources for play spaces; sporting self-directed play; help children and young people to manage risk during play.

Further reading

Bruce, T. (2001) *Helping Young Children Learn Through Play.* Hodder & Stoughton.

Conteh, J. (ed) (2006) *Promoting Learning for Bilingual Pupils 3–11: Opening Doors to Success.* Sage Publications Ltd.

Dunn, K. et al (2003) *Developing Accessible Play Space: A Good Practice Guide.* ODPM. [Available free online at: **www.communities.gov.uk**]

Kamen, T. (2005) *The Playworker's Handbook.* Hodder Arnold.

Kidsactive (2000) *Side by Side: Guidelines for Inclusive Play.* Kidsactive.

Lindon, J. (2001) *Understanding Children's Play.* Nelson Thornes.

McHugh, N. and Springett, S. (2006) *Display a Creative Curriculum.* Belair Publications Ltd.

National Playing Fields Association, Children's Play Council and Playlink (2000) *Best Play: What Play Provision Should do for Children.* NPFA. [Available free online at: **www.ncb.org.uk**]

Pim, C. (2010) *How to Support Learning English as an Additional Language.* LDA.

Seefeldt, C. (2002) *Creating Rooms of Wonder: Valuing and Displaying Children's Work to Enhance the Learning Process.* Gryphon House.

Smyth, G. (2003) *Helping Bilingual Pupils to Access the Curriculum.* David Fulton Publishers.

Taylor, L. (2006) *Rules of Display: The Essential Guide to Nursery and Primary Classroom Displays.* Hodder Gibson.

12. Supporting special educational needs

This chapter relates to QCF units:

TDA 2.15 Support children and young people with disabilities and special educational needs

HSC 2028 Move and position individuals

HSC 2001 Provide support for therapy sessions.

Supporting pupils with special educational needs (SEN)

You must know, understand and follow the relevant legislation regarding pupils with disabilities and SEN. This includes supporting the school in carrying out its duties towards pupils with SEN and that parents are notified of any decision that SEN provision is to be made for their child.

Legislation relating to pupils with special educational needs

The Education Act 1993 defines children with special educational needs as:

(a) Having a significantly greater difficulty in learning than the majority of children of the same age.

(b) Having a disability which either prevents or hinders the child from making use of educational facilities of a kind provided for children of the same age in schools within the area of the local education authority.

(c) An under five who falls within the definition at (a) or (b) above or would do if special educational provision was not made for the child.

The Special Educational Needs and Disability Act 2001 amends Part 4 of the Education Act 1996 to make further provision against discrimination on the grounds of disability in schools and other educational establishments. This Act strengthens the right of children with special educational needs (SEN) to be educated in mainstream schools where parents want this and the interests of other children can be protected. The Act also requires Local Education Authorities (LEAs) to make arrangements for services to provide parents of children with SEN with advice and information. It also requires schools to inform parents where they are making special educational provision for their child and allows schools to request a statutory assessment of a pupil's SEN (**www.drc-gb.org**).

The Special Educational Needs Code of Practice 2001 gives practical advice to Local Education Authorities, maintained schools and others concerning their statutory duties to identify, assess and provide for children's special educational needs. This code came into effect on 1 January 2002 and re-enforces the right for children with SEN to receive education within a mainstream setting and advocates that schools and LEAs implement a graduated method for the organisation of SEN. The code provides a school-based model of intervention (Early Years Action or School Action, Early Years Action Plus or School Action and Statutory Assessment) for children with special educational needs to enable *all* children to have the opportunities available through inclusive education. Accompanying the code is the *Special Educational Needs Toolkit* which expands on the guidance contained in the code. This toolkit is not law but does provide examples of good practice that LEAs and schools can follow.

Identification, assessment and provision for pupils with SEN

Some children may have been identified as having special educational needs prior to starting school, e.g. children with physical disabilities, sensory impairment or autism. Some children may not be making sufficient progress within the early learning goals/national curriculum targets or may have difficulties which require additional support within the school. Additional support for pupils with SEN in education settings may be provided through Early Years or School Action, Early Years or School Action Plus and Statutory Assessment.

Early Years or School Action

Pupils identified as having special educational needs may require support in addition to the usual provision of the school. The special educational need coordinator (SENCO), in consultation with colleagues and the pupil's parents will decide what additional support is needed to help the pupil to make progress. Additional support at Early Years or School Action may include: the provision of different learning materials or special equipment; some individual or group support provided by support staff (e.g. early years practitioners/nursery nurses or teaching assistants) and devising and implementing an Individual Education Plan (see below).

Early Years or School Action Plus

Pupils with special educational needs may require additional support which involves external support services. The SENCO, in consultation with colleagues, the pupil's parents and other professionals will decide what additional support is needed to help the pupil to make progress. Additional support at Early Years or School Action Plus may include: the provision of specialist strategies or materials; some individual or group support provided by specialist support staff (e.g. early years practitioners/nursery nurses or teaching assistants with additional training in SEN); some individual support provided by other professionals, e.g. physiotherapist, speech and language therapist; access to LEA support services for regular advice on strategies or equipment, e.g. educational psychologist, autism outreach worker and devising and implementing an Individual Education Plan (see below).

Statutory Assessment

A few pupils with SEN in the school may still make insufficient progress through the additional support provided by Early Years or School Action Plus. When a pupil demonstrates significant cause for concern, the SENCO, in consultation with colleagues, the pupil's parents and other professionals already involved in the pupil's support, should consider whether to request a Statutory Assessment by the LEA. The LEA may decide that the nature of the provision necessary to meet the pupil's special educational needs requires the LEA to determine the pupil's special education provision through a statement of special educational needs.

 key words

A statement of special educational needs: the statutory provision that must be made to meet a pupil's special educational needs.

A statement of SEN is set out in six parts:

- Part one: general information about the pupil and a list of the advice the authority received as part of the assessment.
- Part two: the description of the pupil's needs following the assessment.
- Part three: describes all the special help to be given for the pupil's needs.
- Part four: the type and name of the school the pupil should go to and how any arrangements will be made out of school hours or off school premises.
- Part five: describes any non-educational needs the pupil has.
- Part six: describes how the pupil will get help to meet any non-educational needs.

Individual Education Plans (IEP)

All education settings should differentiate their approaches to learning activities to meet the needs of individual pupils. The strategies used to enable individual pupils with SEN to make progress during learning activities should be set out in an IEP whether they receive additional support in the school as part of Early Years Action, Early Years Action Plus or a statement of special educational needs.

A pupil's IEP should identify three or four individual targets in specific key areas, for example, communication, literacy, numeracy or behaviour and social skills. When supporting the teacher in developing individual educational plans, remember to have high expectations of pupils and a commitment to raising their achievement based on a realistic appraisal of children's abilities and what they can achieve. You may be involved in regular reviews of Individual Educational Plans in consultation with the pupil's class teacher/form tutor, the SENCO, the pupil and their parents, e.g. at least three times a year.

A pupil's IEP should include the following information:

- pupil's strengths
- priority concerns
- any external agencies involved
- background information including assessment details and/or medical needs
- parental involvement/pupil participation
- the short-term targets for the pupil
- the provision to be put in place, e.g. resources, strategies, staff, allocated support time
- when the plan is to be reviewed
- the outcome of any action taken.

Documentation and information about the *Special Educational Needs Code of Practice* including Early Years or School Action, Early Years or School Action Plus and Statutory Assessment should be available from the school office or the SENCO.

Individual Education Plan			
Name	Fred Jones	**Stage**	Statutory Assessment
Area/s of Concern	Literacy, Maths, Behaviour	**Year Group / IEP No.**	Year 2, Class 7/ IEP No 2
Class Teacher	Mrs J Smith	**Start Date**	April 2010
Supported by	Mr H Brown (TA)	**Review Date**	June 2010
Proposed Support	Twice a week	**Support Began**	October 2009

Targets to be Achieved:
1. To read / spell c-v-c words with vowel sounds 'a' and 'o'.
2. To understand and use number bonds to 10.
3. To sit still on the mat during class / group sessions.
4. To give verbal answers of more than one word.

Achieved:
1.
2.
3.
4.

Achievement Criteria:
1. Accurate when tested at random on three separate occasions.
2. Use number bonds to answer sums accurately on three separate occasions.
3. Achieved on 6 out of ten occasions over a period of a week.
4. Achieved on 4 occasions.

Possible Resources and Techniques:
1. Wooden / plastic letters. Phonic workbooks. Card games. Computer programs. Tracking. Dictation.
2. Additions games e.g. bingo, snap, dice game. Lists of number bonds for reference. Textbooks / worksheets.
3. Clear expectations of behaviour at story time / discussion time. Reward chart.
4. Open-ended questions.

Possible Strategies to use in Class:
1. Encourage Fred to write the sounds he hears in a spoken word and to read c-v-c words accurately.
2. Set verbal and written questions for practising using number bonds. Provide apparatus for support if needed.
3. Minimise the time spent sitting still at first, gradually build up. Seat Fred away from distractions.
4. Question and answer sessions. Encourage full sentence answers.

Ideas for Support Teacher or Teaching Assistant:
1. Use multi-sensory methods for teaching c-v-c words. Set rhyming activities.
2. Provide practical activities to practise number bonds e.g. find different ways of splitting ten objects.
3. Look at the reward chart with Fred. Praise achievement.
4. Use individual discussion.

Parents / Carers need to:
Make sure the words sent home are practised.
Use money to add to 10p.
Encourage Fred to speak in whole sentences.

Pupil needs to:
Try to apply spellings he has learnt to his own written work.
Try to sit still.
Try to speak in whole sentences.

Figure 12.1: Example of Individual Education Plan

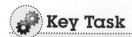 **Key Task**

Outline your school's procedures for ensuring that Individual Education Plans for pupils are in place and regularly reviewed. Provide examples of the relevant forms, e.g. an Individual Education Plan; review sheets for pupil comments, parent comments and staff comments; record of review. Remember confidentiality.

NOS Links:

Level 2:   STL 12.1   STL 12.2   STL 12.3

Roles and responsibilities in supporting pupils with SEN

Supporting pupils with disabilities and/or special educational needs in schools involves establishing the strengths and needs of pupils in partnership with their families and in collaboration with other agencies. It also involves the identification and provision of appropriate resources to enable inclusion and participation.

As a teaching assistant you should contribute to the inclusion of pupils with disabilities and special educational needs. You may be involved in supporting the teacher and the SENCO in developing individual plans to meet each pupil's needs and requesting additional resources or a Statutory Assessment where appropriate.

The role of the special educational needs coordinator

All schools must have a special educational needs coordinator (SENCO) who is the Responsible Person as defined within the *Special Educational Needs Code of Practice*. Pupils with special educational needs require additional support in the school and usually have Individual Education Plans (IEPs). These plans will give information about the support being provided to help the pupil and will include details of the roles and responsibilities of staff members in providing appropriate learning and/or behaviour support. The SENCO is responsible for drawing up these plans, along with the teacher, support staff (e.g. teaching assistant), the pupil and their parents or carers.

The SENCO also has the following responsibilities for managing pupil behaviour and learning:

- To provide support and guidance to all staff to help them manage pupil behaviour and learning effectively.
- To ensure that adequate training is provided to all staff to improve behaviour management strategies and the implementation of learning activities.
- To ensure that (as far as is practical) all resources required are made available to facilitate appropriate learning experiences and effective behaviour management.
- To monitor the changing needs of pupils as they progress through the school.
- To liaise with external agencies.
- To ensure that there are programmes for identifying the needs of new pupils.

The role of the class teacher in supporting pupils with SEN

The class teacher should plan and organise an effective learning environment which: promotes equality, diversity and inclusion (see Chapter 4); promotes positive behaviour (see Chapter 8) and supports *individual* pupil development and learning (see Chapters 1 and 7). The class teacher should carefully monitor pupils' behaviour and learning in order to provide appropriate learning activities. When a pupil experiences difficulties with participating in learning activities and/or behaving appropriately, the class teacher should follow the relevant school strategies.

The class teacher has the following responsibilities for managing pupil behaviour and learning:

- To identify each pupil's needs and skill levels.
- To make the SENCO aware of any concerns about a pupil's behaviour and/or learning.
- To advise the child's parents of any concerns about behaviour and/or learning.
- To provide reports for external agencies.
- To monitor and assess learning/behaviour and maintain appropriate records.
- To fill in and maintain the Special Educational Needs Register.
- To fulfil all other duties required of the class teacher by the *Code of Practice*.
- To ensure the delivery of the curriculum enables *all* pupils, including those with special educational needs, to experience success.

The teaching assistant's role in supporting pupils with SEN

As a teaching assistant you should help pupils with SEN to participate in the full range of activities and experiences (see section on promoting equality, diversity and inclusion in Chapter 4). You need to know and understand the details about particular disabilities or SEN as they affect the pupils in your school. Pupils with additional needs in your school may include pupils with: communication and interaction needs; cognition and learning needs; behavioural, emotional and social development needs; sensory impairment or physical disabilities. (See Further Reading for information about supporting specific special needs.)

Your role may involve supporting a child or young person with special educational needs or additional support needs to participate in activities and experiences offered by the setting in which you work. As well as providing care and encouragement to the child or young person, you will support the family according to your role and the procedures of the setting.

Ten ways to support pupils with special educational needs

You can help pupils with special educational needs to participate in all activities by:

1. Providing a stimulating language-rich childcare environment which is visually attractive, tactile and interactive.
2. Maximising the use of space in the setting to allow freedom of movement for *all* children (including those who are physically disabled or visually impaired).
3. Ensuring accessibility of resources including any specialist equipment.
4. Providing opportunities for all children to explore different materials and activities.
5. Encouraging children to use the abilities they do have to their fullest extent.
6. Providing sufficient time for children to explore their environment and materials; some children may need extra time to complete tasks.
7. Encouraging independence, e.g. use computers, word processing, tape recorders.
8. Praising all children's *efforts* as well as achievements.
9. Supporting families to respond to their children's special needs.
10. Accessing specialist advice and support for children with special needs.

Learning mentors

Learning mentors work with school pupils and college students to help them overcome barriers to learning and so have a better chance of achieving to their potential. Learning mentors play a key role in supporting children and young people with special needs, working closely with teachers and a range of support agencies. Learning mentors use regular one-to-one and group sessions with the pupils/students, to agree targets and strategies (e.g. to improve academic work, attendance, behaviour and relationships). They help pupils/students develop coping strategies, enhance their motivation, raise their aspirations and encourage them to re-engage in learning. Learning mentors should take into account the range of complex issues that are often behind problems with learning and achievement such as bereavement, lack

Figure 12.2: Teaching assistant supporting a pupil with special needs

of confidence/low self-esteem, low aspirations, mental health issues, relationship difficulties, bullying, peer pressure and family issues/concerns. (For more detailed information see section on learning mentors on the Standards website: **www.standards.dfes.gov.uk/learningmentors/**.)

✏️ Activity!

Describe your role and responsibilities for supporting children and/or young people with special educational needs in school.

Liaising with parents regarding their children with SEN

When liaising with parents about the special educational needs of their children you should consider the family's home background and the expressed wishes of the parents. You must also follow the setting's policies and procedures with regard to special educational needs, e.g. inclusion strategies, policies, procedures and practice (see section on understanding children's needs and rights in Chapter 4). You may need to give parents positive reassurance about their children's care and education. Any concerns or worries expressed by a child's parents should be passed immediately to the appropriate person in the school, e.g. the class teacher and/or SENCO. If a parent makes a request to see a colleague or other professional, then you should follow the relevant school policy and procedures. (See section on sharing information with parents and carers in Chapter 3.)

✏️ Activity!

Give examples of how your school exchanges information with parents with regard to their children with special educational needs, e.g. information packs, regular reviews, Individual Education Plans, home-school diaries.

Liaising with other professionals regarding pupils with SEN

The teaching assistant can make a valuable contribution to the school by providing effective support for colleagues and by liaising with parents. In addition, teaching assistants are involved in the network of relationships between staff at the school and other professionals from external agencies such as:

- Local Education Authority, e.g. educational psychologist, special needs support teachers, special needs advisors, specialist teachers, education welfare officers.
- Health services, e.g. paediatricians, health visitors, physiotherapists, occupational therapists, speech and language therapists, play therapists, school nurses, clinical psychologists.
- Social services department, e.g. social workers; specialist social workers: sensory disabilities, physical disabilities, mental health or children and families.
- Charities and voluntary organisations, e.g. AFASIC, British Dyslexia Association, Council for Disabled Children, National Autistic Society, RNIB, RNID, SCOPE.

 **Activity!**

Find out which external agencies and other professionals are connected with the care and support of pupils with SEN at your school.

Pupils with special educational needs will often have support from external agencies. The teaching assistant is part of the educational support team, which also includes the teacher and the **specialist**. To provide the most effective care and support for the pupil, it is essential that the working relationships between the specialist, teacher and teaching assistant run smoothly and that there are no contradictions or missed opportunities due to lack of communication. With guidance from the teacher, teaching assistants can be involved with the work of the specialists in a number of ways: planning support for the pupil with the teacher; assisting pupils to perform tasks set by a specialist and reporting the pupil's progress on such tasks to the teacher.

 key words

Specialist: person with specific training/additional qualifications in a particular area of development, e.g. physiotherapist, speech and language therapist, educational psychologist.

Any interactions with other professionals should be conducted in such a way as to promote trust and confidence in your working relationships. Your contributions towards the planning and implementation of joint actions must be consistent with your role and responsibilities as a teaching assistant in your school. You should supply other professionals with the relevant information, advice and support as appropriate to your own role and expertise. If requested, you should be willing to share information, knowledge or skills with other professionals. You should use any opportunities to contact or observe the practice of professionals from external agencies to increase your knowledge and understanding of their skills/expertise in order to improve your own work in supporting pupil's learning and development.

 **Key Task**

Compile an information booklet suitable for new teaching assistants which includes the following:

- the teaching assistant's role and responsibilities for supporting pupils with special educational needs in the school
- links with other professionals from external agencies established by your school
- liaising with parents and carers
- working with other professionals to support pupils
- sources of further information, e.g. special needs organisations, books, websites.

NOS Links:

Level 2:   **STL 4.1**   **STL 4.2**   **STL 4.3**   **STL 4.4**   **STL 12.1**   **STL 12.2**   **STL 12.3**

Moving and handling pupils with physical disabilities

Part of your role may involve supporting pupils with disabilities by helping them to move and/or reposition themselves. When moving, handling or repositioning pupils, you have a responsibility to do so safely and correctly to ensure your own safety, the pupil's safety and the safety of anyone else in that location. To do this you need to be able to prepare pupils, environments and equipment for moving and handling as well as enabling pupils to move from one position to another.

Activities requiring manual handling

Manual handling (lifting, supporting, carrying, pushing and pulling by bodily force) is one of the most common causes of strain and sprain injury and back pain in people working in all areas of education. Poor manual handling techniques can also result in injury to the pupils.

Some pupils with SEN and/or disabilities may require specialist manual handling, treatment or facilities. Activities which may require manual handling include: moving around school; toileting; playground or outdoor activities; travelling on school transport; activities outside school such as swimming or educational visits and emergency procedures, e.g. moving from the floor after a fall or fire evacuation. Teachers and teacher assistants may have to deal with issues relating to moving and handling pupils that they have not had to address before, for example, when pupils with severe or complex SEN are taught in a mainstream setting or 'special' targeted provision. Some pupils may not be able to recognise everyday hazards, communicate distress or move around independently (HSE, 2006).

Five important points to remember when moving and handling pupils

When moving and handling pupils you should remember these important points:

1. Follow the school's policies and procedures for moving and handling pupils.
2. Identify the steps that need to be taken to manage risk in general terms and the control measures for mobility assistance and other manual handling risks (see sections on risk assessment and manual handling in Chapter 6).

3. Follow the procedures for routine manual handling as well as emergency situations when manual-handling procedures may have to be adapted, e.g. evacuation in the event of a fire.

4. Use the same handling techniques when assisting pupils with moving and handling to ensure consistency and safety as this will help the pupil to remain calm and reduce the possibility of struggling, sudden movement or violence.

5. Ensure that you have received appropriate training in moving and handling including the use of any equipment (e.g. hoists, slides, slings, pillows). You may need refresher training, especially if the needs of the pupil change or you start work with different pupils or in a new setting.

(HSE, 2006)

 Key Task

Describe the role of the teaching assistant in moving and handling pupils with physical disabilities. Include information on your school's procedures for moving and handling pupils during the following activities: moving around school; toileting; playground or outdoor activities; travelling on school transport; activities outside school such as swimming or educational visits; emergency procedures, e.g. moving from the floor after a fall or fire evacuation.

NOS Links:

Level 2:   **STL 12.1**   **STL 12.2**   **STL 12.3**   **STL 13.1**   **STL 13.2**

Supporting pupils during therapy sessions

Your role in supporting pupils with additional needs may also involve providing support during therapy sessions such as behavioural therapy, occupational therapy, physiotherapy or speech and language therapy. This involves working under the direction of a qualified therapist to support them while they run therapy sessions. You may also be involved in supporting the pupil to practise therapy exercises in between the therapy sessions run by the therapist. You will need to support both therapist and pupil before, during and after therapy sessions. To do this you need to be able to prepare and maintain environments, equipment and materials before, during and after therapy sessions. You will also need to support individuals before and during therapy sessions. In addition, you will need to be able to make observations and provide feedback on therapy sessions.

What happens during a therapy session?

What happens during a therapy session depends on: the length of the therapy session; the location of the therapy session; the age of the individual involved; whether the therapy session is individual or involves a group and the type of difficulty or disorder that is being treated. For example, in the first few minutes the therapist may help the pupil to get settled by reviewing what happened in the last session, asking how any practice sessions or 'homework' went and then explaining what will happen in this session. Then the therapist will encourage the pupil to participate in therapeutic activities. During the last few minutes the therapist will discuss with the pupil what needs to be practised for the next session and any 'homework' activities to be completed.

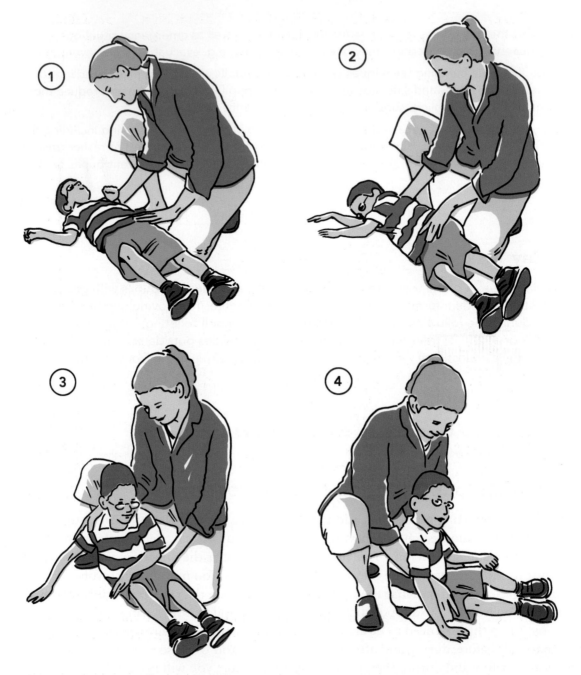

Figure 12.3: Correct procedures for manual handling

Therapy sessions may take place in schools, homes, clinics and/or hospitals. The location where the therapy session takes place will affect the amount of room available and the equipment and materials that can be used. Therapeutic activities should be appropriate to the age and developmental level of the child, with vocabulary and directions which are not too complex for the child to follow. Younger children will have play-based therapeutic activities, while older children may have activities linked to their schoolwork. Most therapy sessions will be either individual or group. Individual sessions allow for more intense personal interaction between the therapist and the child (and possibly the child's parent, carer or assistant) while group sessions can provide children with the same types of difficulties or disorders to participate in different activities such as role play.

Of course, exactly what happens during a therapy session depends on the type of difficulty or disorder being treated. For example, a pupil with communication difficulties may do activities involving flash cards, worksheets, clapping games, practising vocal sounds, story telling or conversation. While a pupil with physical difficulties may have sessions involving massage, therapeutic exercise, mobilisation, stretching and strengthening, improving posture or hydrotherapy. Depending on the age of the pupil, playtime activities and schoolwork may also form the basis for a therapy session.

Figure 12.4: Adult supporting therapy session

Twelve ways to support therapy sessions

You can help to support pupils before, during and after therapy sessions in the following ways:

1. Identifying your role and responsibilities in preparation and addressing any risk and safety requirements including preparing yourself, the environment and materials as instructed.

2. Reporting any damage to materials, equipment or in the environment immediately, and according to organisational procedures and practices.

3. Working with individuals to identify their preferences, concerns and issues about participating in therapy sessions and agree any special requirements.

4. Reassuring individuals about the nature and content of the therapy sessions.

5. Highlighting concerns and issues you are unable to resolve with the therapist, seeking their support to allay the individuals' fears.

6. Supporting specialist practitioners and therapists to run therapy sessions.

7. Following the therapist's directions precisely when carrying out activities that the therapist has delegated to you.

8. Providing active support for individuals within therapy sessions, taking account of their needs, preferences and abilities.

9. Taking appropriate action if the individual has any difficulties and/or you observe any significant changes, e.g. inform your line manager or the therapist, stop the session.

10. Working with individuals and others to review, agree and implement any adjustments that are needed to maximise the individual's participation and the effectiveness of the therapy sessions on their health and social well-being.

11. Following agreed arrangements for the observation of individuals prior to, during and after therapy sessions including checking your observations with appropriate people and against agreed outcomes as well as recording and reporting on therapy sessions within confidentiality agreements and according to legal and organisational requirements.

12. Restoring the environment after the therapy session and clean and store materials according to legal and organisational and safety procedures and agreements.

(TDA, 2007)

 Key Task

Describe the role and responsibilities of the teaching assistant in supporting pupils before, during and after therapy sessions. Include information on the following:

- preparing yourself, the environment and materials
- reporting any damage to the environment or equipment
- following the therapist's directions
- providing reassurance and active support for pupils within therapy sessions
- taking appropriate action if the pupil has any difficulties
- following agreed arrangements for the observation of pupils before, during and after therapy sessions
- restoring the environment after the therapy session.

NOS Links:

Level 2: STL 12.1   STL 12.2   STL 12.3   STL 14.1   STL 14.2   STL 14.3

Summary of the key points in this chapter:

- **Supporting pupils with special educational needs** including legislation relating to pupils with special educational needs.
- **Identification, assessment and provision for pupils with SEN** including: Early Years or School Action; Early Years or School Action Plus; Statutory Assessment; Individual Education Plans.
- **Roles and responsibilities in supporting pupils with SEN** including: the role of the special educational needs coordinator; the role of the class teacher in supporting pupils with SEN; the teaching assistant's role in supporting pupils with SEN; ways to support pupils with special educational needs; learning mentors; liaising with parents regarding their children with SEN; liaising with other professionals regarding pupils with SEN.

- **Moving and handling pupils with physical disabilities** including: activities requiring manual handling; important points to remember when moving and handling pupils.
- **Supporting pupils during therapy sessions** including: what happens during a therapy session; ways to support therapy sessions.

Further Reading

Alcott, M. (2002) *An Introduction to Children with Special Needs.* Hodder & Stoughton.

ATL (2002) *Achievement For All: Working With Children with Special Educational Needs in Mainstream Schools and Colleges.* Association of Teachers and Lecturers. (Available free from: **www.atl.org.uk**)

Autism Working Group (2002) *Autistic Spectrum Disorders: Good Practice Guidance.* DfES. CWDC (2007) *Learning Mentors Practice Guide.* Children's Workforce Development Council. (Available fee at: **www.cwdcouncil.org.uk**)

DfES (2001) *Inclusive Schooling.* DfES. [Available free online from: **http://www.teachernet.gov.uk/_doc/4621/InclusiveSchooling.pdf**]

DfES (2001) *The Special Educational Needs Code of Practice 2001.* DfES.

[Available free at: **http://www.teachernet.gov.uk/_doc/3724/SENCodeOfPractice.pdf**]

Diaz, L. (2008) *The Teaching Assistant's Guide to Speech, Language and Communication Needs.* Continuum International Publishing.

Distin, K. (ed) *Gifted Children: A Guide for Parents and Professionals.* Jessica Kingsley Publishers.

Halliwell, M. (2003) *Supporting Special Educational Needs: A Guide for Assistants in Schools and Pre-schools.* David Fulton Publishers.

HSE (2006) *Health and Safety Matters for Special Educational Needs: Moving and Handling.* Health and Safety Executive. [Available online at: **http://www.hse.gov.uk/pubns/edis4.pdf**]

Lee, C. (2007) *Resolving Behaviour Problems in Your School: A Practical Guide for Teachers and Support Staff.* Paul Chapman Educational Publishing.

Roberts, M. and Constable, D (2003) *Handbook for Learning Mentors in Primary and Secondary Schools.* David Fulton Publishers.

Spohrer, K. (2007) *The Teaching Assistant's Guide to ADHD.* Continuum International Publishing.

Spooner, W. (2006) *The SEN Handbook for Trainee Teachers, NQTs and Teaching Assistants.* Routledge.

Watson, L. et al (2006) *Deaf and Hearing Impaired Pupils in Mainstream Schools.* David Fulton Publishers.

13. Supporting the wider curriculum

This chapter relates to QCF units:

TDA 2.14 Support children and young people at meal or snack times

TDA 2.17 Support children and young people's travel outside the setting

TDA 2.18 Support extra-curricular activities

Supporting children and young people at meal times

Your role may involve supporting children and young people at meal times. This includes: understanding food hygiene and healthy eating (see below); following health and safety procedures (see Chapter 6); supporting children's play (see Chapter 11); managing behaviour (see Chapter 8) and dealing with bullying and safeguarding children (see Chapter 2).

When supporting children and young people at meal times you will be working with others (such as catering staff) to ensure healthy eating and food safety within the setting that enables children and young people to maintain their health and well-being. For example, encouraging growth and development and maintaining a healthy weight through a balanced diet as well as avoiding unnecessary illness, e.g. food poisoning due to poor hygiene.

Basic knowledge of food hygiene

The Chartered Institute of Environmental Health Foundation Certificate in Food Hygiene (formerly Basic Food Hygiene Certificate) is an essential qualification for all food and beverage handlers (including mealtime supervisors in schools, breakfast clubs and after-school clubs providing refreshments) and covers the basic principles of safe food handling. Many colleges include this certificate as part of their training courses. If you do not have this certificate already then the course is available at most local colleges and includes: food poisoning trends and reasons; bacteria and micro-organisms; personal hygiene; food safety legislation; pest control and cleaning and disinfecting.

The setting's procedures for storing and preparing food

You should follow your setting's procedures for storing and preparing food. If you are responsible for the preparation and handling of food you should be aware of, and comply with, regulations relating to food safety and hygiene. For example, if the setting provides meals for children then the kitchen facility must comply with the Food Safety Act 1990 and the Food Safety Regulations 2002. Children should not have access to the kitchen unless it is being used solely for a supervised children's activity.

You can help to maintain food safety by following correct food storage procedures such as:

- Storing the most perishable foods in the coldest part of the fridge.
- Reading and following directions on food package labels about storage, temperature, 'use by' and 'best before' dates.
- Avoiding any possibility of foods dripping onto other food in the fridge (e.g. always store raw meat on a shelf *below* cooked meat and dairy products).
- Keeping eggs in the fridge as warmth will cause deterioration.
- Never keeping or using damaged eggs as eggshells harbour bacteria.
- Maintaining a sufficiently low temperature by avoiding overfilling the fridge.
- Removing unused food from tins, putting in a covered dish, storing in the fridge and using within 48 hours.
- Cooling food quickly before storing in the fridge.
- Storing bread in a bread bin with a tight fitting lid to retain freshness; bread goes stale quickly in the fridge but can be frozen for up to 3 months.
- Keeping food covered, free from flies and other insects and away from any pets.

(Childs, 2001; p. 222)

You should know the relevant areas for eating and drinking in the setting for both yourself and the children and/or young people you work with, for example: the canteen or school hall; designated classroom in a school or room in a community centre; staff may eat with the children/young people or eat their own packed lunches in the staffroom.

 **Activity!**

What are your setting's procedures for the preparation and storage of food?

Providing a satisfying, varied and balanced diet

Depending on the type of setting, you may need to provide regular drinks and food for the children and/or young people. Children attending the setting for a full day should be offered a midday meal or a packed lunch that can be provided by parents. Fresh drinking water should be available to children at all times. Any food and drink provided by the setting should be properly prepared, nutritious and comply with any special dietary requirements.

Healthy eating involves getting the right nutrients from a satisfying, varied and balanced diet. Children and adults need these nutrients to enable their bodies to work efficiently: carbohydrates, proteins, fats, vitamins and minerals. People also need fibre and water to remove waste products and avoid dehydration.

A balanced diet includes a wide variety of food so that sufficient quantities of the different nutrients are consumed. Ensure that the children understand that healthy eating does not have to be boring as a balanced diet can include foods they enjoy eating. For example, eating biscuits, cakes or crisps is okay in small amounts as long as they also eat plenty of the foods with the nutrients they need the most of, e.g. bread, cereals and potatoes; meat, fish and vegetarian alternatives; milk and dairy products; fruit and vegetables.

You should help children and young people to learn about the guidelines for a healthy, balanced diet: enjoy eating food; eat a variety of different foods; eat the right amount to be a healthy weight; eat plenty of foods rich in starch and fibre; eat plenty of fruit and vegetables; do not eat too many foods that contain lots of fat; do not have sugary foods or drinks too often and drink plenty of water (BNF, 2003). You can help children and young people to learn about a healthy, balanced diet through activities such as drawing their own pictures or designing posters or leaflets about a balanced diet.

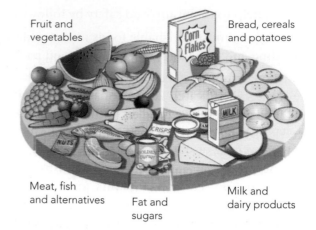

Figure 13.1: A balanced diet

 **Activity!**

Design a poster or leaflet illustrating the guidelines for a healthy, balanced diet. If possible encourage an individual or small group of children/young people to design their own posters or leaflets.

Special dietary requirements

If your setting provides meals and/or snacks and drinks for children then their parents should be requested to give information on any special dietary requirements, preferences or food allergies the child may have. A record should be made of this information during the registration process and the relevant staff should be aware of, and follow, these requirements.

Remember that children from some families may follow strict rules about religious dietary requirements. For example: Jews do not eat pork or shellfish and many only eat *kosher* foods; Muslims do not eat pork and many will eat only *halal* foods; Hindus and Sikhs do not eat beef or are vegetarians/vegans; some Buddhists are also vegetarians. Find out if they are required to follow a certain diet during specific religious festivals, e.g. Muslims who have reached puberty (or 15 years of age) are required to fast from sunrise to sunset during Ramadan. If you are celebrating the cultural diversity of the setting by preparing and sharing foods from different cultures, check whether the children are allowed to do this.

Children from some families are vegetarian or vegan not for religious reasons but as part of their lifestyle choices. You must also be aware of the special dietary requirements of children with food allergies, especially those that can be potentially life threatening, such as a peanut allergy. You should also be aware of the children's individual food preferences and any food their parents do not wish them to eat.

In Practice

Peter has been asked to help prepare a snack for the pupils in the after-school club. One pupil has an allergy to dairy products, two pupils are strict vegetarians and one pupil is reluctant to eat fruit. What kind of healthy and nutritious snack could you prepare in this situation?

Consulting children on the selection and preparation of food and drink

Consulting children/young people on the selection and preparation of food encourages their independence and decision-making skills. Involving them in helping to serve meals or snacks and clearing away afterwards also encourages their independence, as well as helping them take responsibility for looking after their environment. Always follow any health and safety regulations as well as your setting's procedures for these activities.

Encourage the children to try a variety of different foods but be careful not to force them to eat. Remember some children eat more than others and the same child may eat differing amounts at different times, e.g. may eat less if tired, ill or upset or may eat more after energetic play or during a growth spurt. Many children prefer plain and familiar food they can eat with their fingers, but they also need opportunities to develop the skills of using a spoon, fork and then knife. You should encourage children to use safe, child-sized versions of these as appropriate to their age, level of development and culture.

If possible, eat with the children and use the time to share the events of the day so far. Mealtimes should be pleasant and social occasions. Eating with adults provides children with a positive role model, e.g. seeing you enjoying food and trying new foods, observing table manners, etc.

Activity!

Give examples of how children/young people could be involved in the planning and preparation of a meal or snack as appropriate to their ages/levels of development and the procedures of the setting.

Key Task

Describe your involvement in supporting children and young people at meal times. Include information on the following: food hygiene and healthy eating; following health and safety procedures; supporting children's play; managing behaviour; dealing with bullying; safeguarding children.

NOS Links:

Level 2:   **STL 3.1**   **STL 3.2**   **STL 3.3**   **STL 3.4**   **STL 15.1**   **STL 15.2**   **STL 15.3**

Supporting travel out of setting

Part of your role may include supporting travel out of setting involving children and young people with adult supervision, e.g. for home-to-school travel, educational visits, field studies or sports fixtures. This may involve organising and supervising travel for children, young people and adults. Travel may be 'self-powered', e.g. on foot or by bicycle, in an owned or hired vehicle or by public transport (TDA, 2007).

To ensure pupil safety you must follow the school's policy and procedures for supporting travel out of setting including:

- collecting the relevant information for the pupils to be escorted
- ensuring the staff/pupil ratio meets organisational and legal requirements
- ensuring that everyone involved is aware of the travel arrangements
- ensuring that staff are at the meeting point at the agreed time
- escorting the pupils in a safe manner using the agreed route and mode of transport
- ensuring the pupils enter the setting in a safe manner
- carrying out the agreed procedures for pupils who are not at the meeting point.

Figure 13.2: Poster promoting healthy eating in school

 Key Task

Describe your setting's policy and procedures for organising and supervising travel.

NOS Links:

Level 2:   STL 3. 1   STL 3.2

Helping to supervise pupils on educational trips and out-of-school activities

The health and safety of pupils on educational visits is part of the school's overall health and safety policy. The most senior member of staff on the educational visit will usually have overall responsibility and act as the group leader. Any other teachers present will also have responsibility for pupils on educational visits at all times. Teaching assistants on educational visits should be clear about their exact roles and responsibilities during any visit.

Teaching assistants helping to supervise pupils on educational visits must:

- follow the instructions of the group leader and teacher supervisors
- not have sole charge of pupils (unless previously agreed as part of the risk assessment for the visit)
- help to maintain the health and safety of everyone on the visit
- help with the control and discipline of pupils to avoid potential dangers/accidents

- never be alone with a pupil wherever possible (this is for the protection of both the adult and the pupil)
- report any concerns about the health or safety of pupils to the group leader or teacher supervisors immediately.

(DfEE, 1998)

Teaching assistants should be aware of pupils who might require closer supervision during educational visits (e.g. pupils with special educational needs or behavioural difficulties). Additional safety procedures to those used in school may be necessary to support pupils with medical needs during educational visits (e.g. arrangements for taking medication). Sometimes it might be appropriate to ask the parent or a care assistant to accompany the pupil to provide extra help and support during the visit.

Organising emergency procedures is a fundamental part of planning an educational visit. All participants, including staff, pupils and parents, should know who will take charge in an emergency during the educational visit and what their individual responsibilities are in the event of an emergency. The group leader would usually take charge in an emergency and must ensure that emergency procedures including back up cover have been arranged. (See section on dealing with accidents and injuries in Chapter 6.)

Ten Golden Rules for maintaining pupil safety during educational visits

All outings with pupils should be both safe and enjoyable, so to make this possible you should work with the teacher and follow these ten golden rules:

1. Check the educational visit is suitable for the ages and levels of development of the pupils participating.
2. Obtain written permission from the children's parents.
3. Ensure the destination, leaving time and expected return times are written down.
4. Know how to get there, e.g. location, route and mode of transport.
5. Check the seasonal conditions, weather and time available.
6. Assess any potential dangers or risks, e.g. activities near water, suitability and safety of playground equipment.
7. Carry essential information/equipment such as identification, emergency contact numbers, mobile phone, first aid, spare clothing, food, money and any essential medication.
8. Make sure you and the pupils are suitably dressed for the occasion, e.g. sensible shoes or boots for walks; waterproof clothing for wet weather; sunhat and sun screen in hot weather; clean, tidy clothes for cinema, theatre, museum visits, etc.
9. Ensure the correct number of children is accountable throughout the outing.
10. All participants, including staff, children and parents, should know who will take charge in an emergency during the outing and what their individual responsibilities are in the event of an emergency (see Chapter 6).

Figure 13.3: Teaching assistant with pupils on educational visit

 Key Task

1. Outline your role and responsibilities with regard to maintaining pupil safety during educational visits and out-of-school activities.
2. Give a reflective account of your involvement on an educational visit.

NOS Links:

Level 2: STL 1.1   STL 3. 1   STL 3.2   STL 3.3   STL 3.4   STL 4.1   STL 4.2   STL 4.3   STL 4.4   STL 10.1   STL 10.5

Supporting extra-curricular activities

You may be involved in providing support for extra-curricular activities for children and/or young people to develop their skills and talents, e.g. through sporting, musical, artistic, creative, intellectual or linguistic activities. Extra-curricular activities include clubs, sports teams, recreational activities or performing arts groups which are under the direction of the school but with limited supervision. When supporting extra-curricular activities you will need to help with preparing children and/or young people for the activity and supporting the children and/or young people during the activity.

Preparing children and young people for an extra-curricular activity

When preparing children and young people for an extra-curricular activity, you should help the leader of the activity to:

- help the children/young people to feel welcome and at ease
- follow your school's procedures for checking the children/young people present

- ensure the children/young people's dress and equipment are safe and appropriate
- organise the children/young people so they can communicate effectively with them
- explain the aims and content of the session to the children/young people
- find out if the children/young people have any relevant experience you could build on
- ensure the children/young people are mentally and physically prepared for the activity, e.g. doing warm-up exercises
- check that the children/young people understand what to do
- motivate the children/young people to take part without putting them under pressure.

(TDA, 2007)

 Key Task

Describe how you have helped to prepare children and/or young people for an extra-curricular activity. Include information on: the setting; the type of activity; the ages of the children/young people; health and safety requirements, e.g. appropriate and safe clothes and equipment; organisation of the activity; warm-up exercises.

NOS Links:

Level 2:   STL 3.1   STL 4.1   STL 4.3   **and depending on the activity:**
           STL 10.1   STL 10.2   STL 10.3   STL 10.4   STL 10.5   STL 15.1
           STL 15.2   STL 15.3

Providing support during an extra-curricular activity

When supporting children and young people during an extra-curricular activity, you should:

- Make sure the children/young people are following instructions throughout the activity.
- Give the children/young people clear and supportive feedback at appropriate points.
- Provide the children/young people with additional explanations and demonstrations when necessary.
- Encourage the children/young people to say how they feel about the activity and respond to their feelings appropriately.

Figure 13.4: Adult supporting pupils during an extra-curricular activity

- Communicate and interact with the children/young people in a way that is appropriate to their age, stage of development and needs.
- Give adequate attention to each child/young person in the group, according to their needs.
- Encourage effective communication and inter-personal skills between the children/young people.
- Encourage and support the children/young people to consider the impact of their behaviour on others, themselves and their environment.

- Highlight and praise types of behaviour that have a positive effect on the group as a whole.
- Identify and challenge inappropriate behaviour in a way that maintains the emotional welfare of the children/young people and follows agreed procedures.
- Establish and maintain a relationship with the children/young people consistent with the situation and ethical requirements.

(TDA, 2007)

 Key Task

Give examples of how you have supported children and/or young people during an extra-curricular activity. Include information on: the setting; the type of activity; the ages and developmental needs of the children/young people; providing feedback to the children/young people; communication and interaction with children/young people; encouraging positive behaviour; dealing with inappropriate behaviour.

NOS Links:

Level 2:   **STL 3.3**   **STL 3.4**   **STL 4.1**   **STL 4.3**   **and depending on the activity:** **STL 10.1**   **STL 10.2**   **STL 10.3**   **STL 10.4**   **STL 10.5**   **STL 15.1**   **STL 15.2**   **STL 15.3**

Summary of key points in this chapter:

- **Supporting children and young people at meal times** including: basic knowledge of food hygiene; the setting's procedures for storing and preparing food; providing a satisfying, varied and balanced diet; special dietary requirements; consulting children on the selection and preparation of food and drink.
- **Supporting travel out of setting** including: helping to supervise pupils on educational trips and out-of-school activities; maintaining pupil safety during educational visits.
- **Supporting extra-curricular activities** including: preparing children and young people for an extra-curricular activity; providing support during an extra-curricular activity.

Further Reading

Childs, C. (2001) *Food and Nutrition in the Early Years*. Hodder & Stoughton.

Dare, A. and O'Donovan, M. (2002) *A Practical Guide to Child Nutrition*. 2nd Edition. Nelson Thornes.

DfEE (1998) *Health and Safety of Pupils on Educational Visits: A Good Practice Guide*. DfEE.

DfES (2006) *Learning Outside the Classroom*. DfES.

Gamlin, L. (2005) *The Allergy Bible*. 2nd Edition. Quadrille Publishing Ltd.

Rose, S. (2009) *A Handbook of Lunchtime Supervision*. 2nd edition. Routledge.

Scottish Executive (2006) *Nutritional Guidance for Early Years: Food Choices for Children Aged 1 – 5 Years in Early Education and Childcare Settings*. Scottish Executive. [Available free online: **www.scotland.gov.uk**]

14. Supporting assessment for learning

This chapter relates to QCF units:

TDA 2.9 Support assessment for learning

Assessment for learning

Supporting assessment for learning involves using assessment, as part of the teaching and learning process, to raise pupil achievement. This includes using assessment strategies, as agreed with the teacher, to promote learning, such as observing pupils and helping pupils to review their own learning and identify their own learning needs.

You will also need to know and follow the school's procedures for maintaining pupil records including: the range of pupil records; record keeping systems and procedures; the roles and responsibilities for record keeping; storing records; record keeping and confidentiality and legal implications and restrictions.

You may be involved in invigilating external and internal tests and examinations under formal conditions including module tests, practical and oral examinations. This includes preparing the examination room and any resources, bringing candidates into the room and running the test or examination session according to the centre's procedures. You will also need to know how to deal with specific situations such as access arrangements, emergencies and suspicion of malpractice.

As well as being able to observe children's development (see Chapter 1) you also need to help the teacher assess children's development based on observational findings and other reliable information from pupils, parents, carers, colleagues and other appropriate adults. You must be able to make formative and summative assessments (see below) and record your assessments as appropriate to the policies and procedures of your school. You should share your findings with pupils and their parents as appropriate to your role. You should also refer any concerns about pupils to the teacher, senior colleagues and/or relevant external agencies when required. Always remember to follow the school's confidentiality and record keeping requirements (see section below on maintaining pupil records).

Assessment for learning involves using assessment, as part of teaching and learning, in ways that will raise pupils' achievement. The characteristics of assessment for learning are that it:

- is embedded in a view of teaching and learning of which it is an essential part
- involves sharing learning goals with pupils
- aims to help pupils to know and to recognise the standards they are aiming for
- involves pupils in self-assessment
- provides feedback which leads to pupils recognising their next steps and how to take them
- is underpinned by confidence that every pupil can improve
- involves both teacher and pupils reviewing and reflecting on assessment information.

(TDA, 2007)

Assessment strategies are the approaches and techniques used for on-going assessment during lessons or learning activities, such as: using open-ended questions; observing pupils; listening to how pupils describe their work and their reasoning; checking pupils' understanding and engaging pupils in the reviewing progress.

Formative and summative assessments

Formative assessments are initial and on-going assessments. Formative assessments identify learning goals for individuals and groups as appropriate to the ages, developmental needs and abilities of pupils *and* the requirements of the school. Formative assessments are continuous and inform planning provision to promote children's development and learning. Examples of formative assessments include: pupil observations; tick charts/lists; reading records; maths records and daily target records for pupils with Individual Education Plans.

Formative assessment involves observing pupils, monitoring pupils' work, providing oral feedback and informative and critical marking.

Critical marking allows pupils to:

- appreciate their own performance
- find and correct their own mistakes
- identify their own strengths and weaknesses
- receive praise and rewards for their efforts
- be motivated by seeing that their work is valued.

Critical marking allows teachers and teaching assistants to:

- respond consistently in acknowledging pupils' work
- recognise effort and progress as well as attainment
- respond positively, constructively and sympathetically
- involve pupils in the marking process, whenever possible
- monitor the performance of individuals and groups of pupils
- set targets as and when appropriate
- tell the pupils what they need to do next to progress
- make an assessment of pupils' achievement
- develop their curriculum planning
- inform parents about their children's progress.

key words

Critical marking: specific and helpful comments to encourage and extend learning e.g. rather than just stating 'Good work', giving an explanation as to why such as 'Good work with appropriate vocabulary and correct punctuation. Remember to check your spelling. Your handwriting is neat and readable. Well done!'.

Formative assessments: are initial and on-going assessments that identify future targets for pupils as appropriate to their ages, developmental needs and abilities.

Learning goals: are the personalised learning targets for individual pupils. Learning goals relate to learning objectives (what the teacher intends the pupils to learn) and take account of the past achievements and current learning needs of the pupil.

Summative assessments are assessments that summarise findings. Summative assessments involve more formal monitoring of pupil progress. Summative assessments should be used appropriately and allow judgements to be made about each pupil's achievement. Summative assessments are usually in the form of criterion-based tests or tasks. Examples of summative assessments include: Foundation Stage Profile; Standard Assessment Tasks (SATs); teacher assessments; annual school reports; reviews of pupils with special educational needs. (See also the section on providing information on pupil progress and responses in Chapter 7.)

key words

Summative assessments: are assessments that summarise findings and involve more formal monitoring of pupil progress that allow judgements to be made about each pupil's level of achievement.

Curriculum frameworks and assessment requirements

You need to know the relevant school curriculum and age-related expectations of pupils in the subject/curriculum area and age range of the pupils with whom you are working. For example, in England the relevant curricula are The Early Years Foundation Stage and the National Curriculum. (Information about curriculum frameworks is in Chapter 7.)

The Practice Guidance for the Early Years Foundation Stage provides detailed formative assessment suggestions in the 'Look, listen and note' sections of the areas of learning and development. Early years practitioners should: make systematic observations and assessments of each child's achievements, interests and learning styles; use these observations and assessments to identify learning priorities and plan relevant and motivating learning experiences for each child and match their observations to the expectations of the early learning goals. The Early Years Foundation Stage Profile is a way of summing up each child's development and learning achievements at the end of the EYFS. It is based on practitioners' ongoing observation and assessments in all six areas of learning and development. Each child's level of development must be recorded against the 13 assessment scales derived from the early learning goals. Judgements against these scales, which are set out in Appendix 1 of the *Statutory Framework for the Early Years Foundation Stage*, should be made from observation of consistent and independent behaviour, predominantly children's self-initiated activities (**www.standards.dfes.gov.uk/eyfs**).

During Key Stages 1 to 3, pupil progress in most National Curriculum subjects is assessed against eight levels. At the end of Key Stage 1 each pupil's level of attainment is based on the teacher's assessment of reading, writing, speaking and listening, mathematics and science which take into account the pupil's performance in several tasks and tests in reading, writing (including handwriting and spelling) and mathematics. By the age of seven years most pupils are expected to reach Level 2. At the end of Key Stage 2 each pupil's level of attainment is based on the teacher's assessment and the pupil's performance in the national tests in English, Mathematics and Science. By the age of eleven years most pupils are expected to reach Level 4. In Key Stage 3 each pupil's level of attainment is based on the teacher's assessment of: English; Mathematics; Science; Information and Communication Technology; Design and Technology; History; Geography; Art and Design; Music; Physical Education, Citizenship; Modern Foreign Languages; Religious Education. By the age of fourteen most pupils are expected to achieve Level 5. In Key Stage 4 each pupil's attainment is assessed by GCSE levels of achievement at age 16 (Year 11) in the compulsory subjects of English, Mathematics, Science, Information and Communication Technology, Physical Education and Citizenship as well as the pupil's chosen subjects in the entitlement curriculum areas (e.g. the arts, Design and Technology, Humanities and Modern Foreign Languages). At the end of Key Stage 4 most pupils are expected to attain at least 5 GCSEs at Grades A–D.

Further information about curriculum assessment in England is available at:

http://www.qcda.gov.uk/assessment/82.aspx.

Information about curriculum assessment in Northern Ireland is available at:

http://www.nicurriculum.org.uk/foundation_stage/assessment/assessment_for_learning.asp.

Information about curriculum assessment in Scotland is available at:

http://www.ltscotland.org.uk/curriculumforexcellence/assessmentandachievement/index.asp.

Information about curriculum assessment in Wales is available at:

http://wales.gov.uk/topics/educationandskills/curriculumassessment/?lang=en.

 **Activity!**

Find out about the curriculum framework and assessment requirements applicable to the pupils you work with.

Supporting pupils to review their own learning

When supporting assessment for learning you need to support pupils to review their own learning and identify their own emerging learning needs. You can do this by:

- Using information gained from monitoring pupil participation and progress to help pupils to review their learning strategies, achievements and future learning needs.
- Providing time for pupils to reflect upon what they have learnt and to identify where they still have difficulties.
- Listening carefully to pupils and positively encouraging them to communicate their needs and ideas for future learning.
- Supporting pupils in using peer assessment and self-assessment to evaluate their learning achievements.
- Supporting pupils to reflect on their learning, identify the progress they have made and identify their emerging learning needs.
- Supporting pupils to identify the strengths and weaknesses of their learning strategies and plan how to improve them.

(TDA, 2007)

Ashwood Park Primary School

CHILD'S RESULTS

End of key stage 2 assessment results 2003

Name: Thomas Jennings   Class: 6B

ENGLISH

Teachers assessment results

Speaking and listening	level 4
Reading	level 5
Writing	level 5
English result	**level 5**

Test results

Reading	level 5
Writing	level 5
English result	**level 5**

MATHEMATICS

Teacher assessment result	level 4
Test result	level 4

SCIENCE

Teacher assessment result	level 4
Test result	level 5

Level 3 and below represent achievement below the nationally expected standard for most 11-year-olds. Level 4 represents achievement at the nationally expected standard for most 11-year-olds. Levels 5 and 6 represent achievement above the nationally expected standards for most 11-year-olds.

Figure 14.1: Example of assessment sheet

 Key Task

- What is the curriculum framework applicable to the pupils you work with?
- What are the assessment requirements applicable to the pupils you work with? Provide examples of any assessment sheets you use.
- What are your role and responsibilities in the assessment process?
- List examples of how you support pupils to review their own learning and identify their own emerging learning needs.

NOS Links:

Level 2:   STL 1.3   STL 4.4   STL 9.1   STL 9.2   STL 14.3

Level 3:   STL 30.1   STL 30.2

Supporting assessment for learning   223

School reports

In education settings it is a legal requirement that parents receive a written report at least once a year detailing the progress of their children in the National Curriculum subjects plus RE. General comments should also be made concerning the child's general progress and behaviour along with other achievements in the school including extra-curricular activities. All relevant personnel should be encouraged to contribute to these reports. School reports also contain teacher assessment and test level or examination results at the end of each key stage according to current statutory requirements. Each report must also detail the number of authorised and unauthorised absences since the last report.

A pupil's annual report should:

- Be written clearly and concisely without too much jargon.
- Summarise the pupil's performance since the last report.
- Outline the pupil's level of attainment in the National Curriculum subjects. National Curriculum levels of attainment are required only in the core subjects in Years 2, 6 and 9. However, parents are informed if their child is working below, at or above National Curriculum levels in the remaining year groups. For pupils in Key Stage 4, the school report will outline the pupil's expected GCSE results (Year 10) and actual GCSE results (Year 11).
- Set out what the pupil has actually learned, not just what they have been taught during the school year.
- Highlight positive achievements and progress made by the pupil.
- Identify the pupil's weaknesses and suggest positive future action.
- Set realistic targets to motivate the pupil for the coming school year.

Each report should be shared with the pupil who should be encouraged to comment on their own progress in writing where possible. Reports are usually given to parents in July and staff should be available to discuss pupil reports by appointment at a special parents' evening arranged for this purpose. Parents should be invited to write comments about their children's reports on a separate slip that is returned to and kept by the school along with a copy of each report.

 **Activity!**

- Outline your school's policy and procedures for reporting pupil progress to parents.
- What are your responsibilities for reporting pupil progress to parents?

Maintaining pupil records

As a teaching assistant, you will help with classroom records under the close supervision of the teacher responsible for maintaining them. This includes helping with the range of written records used within the school to monitor individual pupils, learning activities, classroom resources and requisitions.

Pupil's Name *Thomas Jennings*   **Class** *6B*

Teacher *Miss Basterfield*

Attendance: Sessions School Open | 336 |
                   Attendance | 99.9% |
                   Unauthorised Absence | 0% |

General Progress and Attitude: Tom had an unsteady start to the year, with his attitude and attention towards his work fluctuating. This often resulted in the production of work that didn't always reflect his true capabilities. Fortunately the challenge of SATs and Tom's developing maturity have led to Tom adopting a more consistent approach to his daily work. Tom is learning the value of concentrated attention and he has developed a sense of pride in his work. Although Tom occasionally allows himself to become distracted, he is much more focused and has the ability to do well in all aspects of the curriculum

Target: I hope that Tom continues to develop a sense of pride in his work and is able to work for sustained periods, without distraction.

I have read what my teacher has written about me.

Child's Signature   *Tom Jennings*

Teacher's Signature   *Ruth Basterfield.*

Headteacher's Signature

C:\serif\pp30\report.ppp

Figure 14.2: Example of school report

The range of pupil records

All schools keep records of essential personal information for each pupil including: home address and telephone number; emergency information, e.g. names and contact telephone numbers for parents/guardians/carers, GP; medical history and conditions such as allergies; cultural or religious practices which may have implications for the care and education of the pupil such as special diets, exclusion from R E and assemblies; who collects the pupil (if applicable) including the transport arrangements (such as taxi or minibus) for a pupil with special educational needs. Schools also have records relating to administrative duties, for example, permission slips for educational visits and requisition forms for school supplies.

Schools also have education records relating to the assessment of pupil progress and their achievements within the National Curriculum framework. Formative assessments include: reading records; maths records; tick charts/lists; observation sheets and daily target records for pupils with Individual Education Plans. Summative assessments include: class teacher assessments; SATs results; pupils' annual school reports and reviews of pupils with SEN.

 **Activity!**

Describe the range of pupil records. If possible, give examples of the types of pupil records used for the pupils with whom you work.

Record keeping systems and procedures

Record keeping systems and procedures are essential to: monitor pupil progress; provide accurate and detailed information regarding pupils' learning and behaviour; determine the effectiveness of an activity or target; determine the effectiveness of adult support or intervention; give constructive feedback to the pupil; share information with the teacher, other professionals and parents and identify and plan for new learning objectives or behaviour targets.

The record keeping systems and procedures you need to follow will depend on the planning and assessment requirements of the school, the class/subject teacher, the SENCO and any other professionals involved in meeting the pupils' educational needs. It is important to update records on a regular basis; the frequency of updating depends on the different types of records that you make a contribution towards. Records that may indicate potential problems with individual pupils should be shown to the class teacher (e.g. observations of unacceptable behaviour; daily records which show poor performance).

 **Activity!**

Find out about the record keeping systems and procedures used within your school.

Roles and responsibilities for record keeping

As a teaching assistant, most of your work with pupils will be planned by others, for example, the class/subject teacher, the SENCO or relevant specialists. They will need regular information about your work, such as updates about a particular pupil's progress. Where, when and how to record pupil information should be directed by the teacher. For example, when recording a pupil's behaviour using time or event sampling, you will need to agree on specific dates and times on which observations will take place. Some information may be given orally, for example outlining a pupil's progress on a particular activity or commenting on a pupil's behaviour.

Spoken information needs to be given in a professional manner, that is: to the appropriate person (class or subject teacher or SENCO); in the right place (not in a corridor where confidential information could be overheard) and at the right time (urgent matters need to be discussed with the class or subject teacher immediately while others may wait until a team meeting).

Requests for records or reports should be dealt with professionally and handed in on time. This is particularly important if the information is needed for a meeting or review as any delay may stop others from performing their responsibilities effectively. Always remember to maintain confidentiality as appropriate to the school's requirements (see below).

 Key Task

- Find out about the school's record keeping policy. Highlight the responsibilities of the teaching assistant as set out in this policy.
- What are your role and responsibilities in maintaining pupil records? With the teacher's permission include: copies of individual pupil records, e.g. literacy and numeracy records, Foundation Stage profile, individual education plans (IEPs), behaviour support plans/logs and copies of school or class records, e.g. registers, educational visit documentation, with your comments about your involvement.

NOS Links:

Level 2:   **STL 1.3**   **STL 4.4**   **STL 5.1**   **STL 9.1**   **STL 9.2**   **STL 14.3**

Storing records

You need to know the exact policy and procedures for storing records in the school. You should also know what your own role and responsibilities are regarding the storage of records. Most pupil and staff records are stored and locked away in a central location such as the school office. Some formative records that need to be accessed or updated on a regular basis may be kept in the pupils' classrooms.

You must maintain the safe and secure storage of school records at all times. You should not leave important documents lying around; always put them back in storage after use. As well as the physical security of records, you need to be aware of the levels of staff access to information. You should never give out the passwords to school equipment (e.g. computers) unless you have permission from the member of staff responsible for the record keeping systems.

 **Activity!**

What is the school policy for the storage and security of pupil records?

Record keeping and confidentiality

Confidentiality is important with regard to record keeping and the storing of information; only the appropriate people should have access to confidential records. Except where a pupil is potentially at risk, information should not be given to other agencies unless previously agreed. Where the passing of confidential information is acceptable then it should be given in the agreed format. Always follow the school policy and procedures regarding confidentiality and the sharing of information; check with the teacher (or your line manager) if you have any concerns about these matters.

Legal implications and restrictions

You should be aware of any legal requirements with regard to record keeping in the school. These include the Data Protection Act 1998, the Children Act 1989, the Education Act 2002, the Race Relations Act 1976 and the SEN Code of Practice 2001. In particular, you need to be aware of the basic legal requirements concerning the recording and filing of personal information under the Data Protection Act 1998 (see section on confidentiality matters in Chapter 3).

There are some circumstances where access to educational records may be restricted:

'The Secretary of State may by order exempt from the subject information provisions, or modify those provisions in relation to personal data in respect of which the data controller is the proprietor of, or a teacher at, a school, and which consist of information relating to persons who are or have been pupils at the school...' (Section 30 (2) Data Protection Act, 1998).

Activity!

- What are the basic legal requirements concerning the recording and filing of personal information under The Data Protection Act 1998?
- What are the school's confidentiality requirements with regard to record keeping? Highlight the responsibilities of the teaching assistant as set out in this policy.
- Outline your main responsibilities for maintaining the confidentiality of pupil information.

Invigilating tests and examinations

Part of your role may include invigilating external or internal tests and examinations, including module tests and practical and oral examinations, under formal conditions. This involves running tests and examinations in the presence of the candidates and includes: preparing the examination room and resources; bringing candidates into the room and running the test or examination session according to the centre's procedures. You will also need to know how to deal with specific situations such as: access arrangements for pupils with special needs, e.g. reading assistance, scribe, sign interpreter; emergencies, e.g. illness or fire evacuation and suspicion of malpractice, e.g. cheating.

In Practice

Francesca is working with pupils aged 15 to 16 who are sitting a module test for mathematics which includes a non-calculator paper. How would you deal with each of the following situations?

- a pupil with dyslexia
- a pupil who is taken ill during the test
- a pupil who appears to be using a calculator.

Invigilating tests and examinations may involve:

- Assisting with making public examinations entries and receiving and processing results.
- Assisting with the organisation of public examinations before, during and after each session.
- Assisting with the administration of school examinations.
- Ensuring the requirements for the conduct of tests and examinations are met, e.g. the required number and positioning of desks/ work stations, display of notices, seating plan, clock, centre number, instructions for candidates and attendance register.

Figure 14.3: Adult invigilating school examination

- Considering health and safety arrangements and environmental conditions such as heating, lighting, ventilation and the level of outside noise.
- Meeting specific requirements, such as additional requirements in relation to further guidance, erratum notices, supervision of individual candidates between tests or examinations and access arrangements for candidates with additional needs.
- Being responsible for the issue of certificates and archives.
- Producing the school's examination statistics.

Key Task

Outline your role and responsibilities for invigilating tests and examinations. Include information on the following:

- the policy, procedures and regulations applicable to tests and examinations in your school
- how you prepare to run tests and examinations
- how you implement and maintain invigilation requirements.

NOS Links:

Level 2 and Level 3: STL17.1 STL17.2

Summary of key points in this chapter:

- **Assessment for learning** including: formative and summative assessments; curriculum frameworks and assessment requirements; supporting pupils to review their own learning; school reports.
- **Maintaining pupil records** including the range of pupil records; record keeping systems and procedures; the roles and responsibilities for record keeping; storing records; record keeping and confidentiality; legal implications and restrictions.
- **Invigilating tests and examinations** including running tests and examinations in the presence of the candidates under formal conditions.

Further Reading

Balshaw, M. and Farrell, P. (2002) *Teaching Assistants: Practical Strategies for Effective Classroom Support*. David Fulton Publishers.

CCEA (2009) *Assessment for Learning: A Practical Guide*. Council for the Curriculum Examinations and Assessment. **http://www.nicurriculum.org.uk/docs/assessment_for_learning/AfL_A%20 Practical%20Guide.pdf**

Dean, J. (2005) *The Teaching Assistant's Guide to Primary Education*. Routledge Falmer.

DfES (2005) *Working Together: Teaching Assistants and Assessment for Learning*. DfES.

DfES (2007) *Primary and Secondary National Strategies: Pedagogy and Personalisation*. DfES.

Dupree, J. (2005) *Help Students Improve Their Study Skills: A Handbook for Teaching Assistants in Secondary Schools*. David Fulton Publishers Ltd.

Galloway, J. (2004) *ICT for Teaching Assistants*. David Fulton Publishers Ltd.

Hutchin, V. (2007) *Supporting Every Child's Learning Across the Early Years Foundation Stage*. Hodder Murray.

Lindon, J. (2005) *Understanding Child Development: Linking Theory and Practice*. Hodder Arnold.

QCA (2008) *Assessing Pupils' Progress: Assessment at the Heart Of Learning*. Qualifications and Curriculum Authority.

The Scottish Government (2010) *Curriculum for Excellence: Building The Curriculum 5 – A Framework for Assessment*. The Scottish Government.

http://www.ltscotland.org.uk/Images/BtC5_assessment_tcm4-582215.pdf

Welsh Assembly Government (2007) *How to Develop Thinking and Assessment for Learning in the Classroom*. Welsh Assembly Government.

http://wales.gov.uk/dcells/publications/curriculum_and_assessment/ developingthinkingassessment/assessmentforlearning-e.pdf?lang=en

Wyse, D. and Hawtin, A. (1999) *Children: A Multi-Professional Perspective*. Arnold. [Covers child development and learning from birth to 18 years.]

[Note: the DfES publications are available free online at: **www.standards.dfes.gov.uk**]

Bibliography

Abbott, L. and **Langston**, A. (2005) *Birth to Three Matters: Supporting the Framework of Effective Practice.* Milton Keynes: Open University Press.

Alexander, R. et al (2009) *Introducing the Cambridge Primary Review.* Cambridge: University of Cambridge.

ATL (2000) 'ATL guide to children's attitudes' in *Report.* June/July issue. London: Association of Teachers and Lecturers.

ATL (2002) *Achievement For All: Working with Children with Special Educational Needs in Mainstream Schools and Colleges.* London: Association of Teachers and Lecturers.

Ball, C. (1994) *Start Right: The Importance of Early Learning.* London: RSA.

Balshaw, M. and **Farrell**, P. (2002) *Teaching Assistants: Practical Strategies for Effective Classroom Support.* London: David Fulton Publishers.

Bartholomew, L. and **Bruce**, T. (1993) *Getting To Know You: A Guide to Record-Keeping in Early Childhood Education and Care.* London: Hodder & Stoughton.

Becta (2004) *Data Protection and Security: A Summary for Schools.* Coventry: British Educational Communications and Technology Agency.

Becta (2006) British Educational Communications and Technology Agency website: **www.becta.org. uk**

Booth, T. and **Swann**, W. (eds) (1987) *Including Pupils with Disabilities.* Milton Keynes: Open University Press.

Brennan, W.K. (1987) *Changing Special Education Now.* Milton Keynes: Open University Press.

BNF (2003) *The Balance of Good Health.* London: British Nutrition Foundation.

Bruce, T. and **Meggitt**, C. (2002) *Child Care and Education.* 3rd revised edition. London: Hodder Arnold.

Burton, G. and **Dimbleby**, R. (1995) *Between Ourselves: An Introduction to Interpersonal Communication.* Revised edition. London: Hodder Arnold.

CAPT (2002) *Taking Chances: The Lifestyles and Leisure Risks of Young People.* London: Child Accident Prevention Trust.

CAPT (2004a) *Factsheet: Children and Accidents.* London: Child Accident Prevention Trust.

CAPT (2004b) *Factsheet: Playground Accidents.* London: Child Accident Prevention Trust.

CRE (1989) *From Cradle to School: Practical Guide to Race Equality and Childcare.* London: Commission for Racial Equality.

CYPU (2001) *Learning to Listen: Core Principles for the Involvement of Children and Young People.* Children and Young People's Unit. London: DfES.

Childs, C. (2001) *Food and Nutrition in the Early Years.* London: Hodder & Stoughton.

Davies, R. (1984) 'Social development and social behaviour' (see **Fontana**, D.)

DCMS (2004) *Getting Serious About Play: A Review of Children's Play.* London: Department for Culture Media & Sport.

DCSF (2007) *The Early Years Foundation Stage – Effective Practice: Play and Exploration.* London: DCSF.

DCSF (2008a) *Information Sharing: Guidance for Practitioners and Managers.* London: DCSF & Communities and Local Government.

DCSF (2008b) *Practice Guidance for the Early Years Foundation Stage.* Revised edition. London: DCSF.

DCSF (2008c) *Statutory Framework for the Early Years Foundation Stage.* Revised edition. London: DCSF.

DCSF (2009) *Promoting and Supporting Positive Behaviour in Primary Schools: Developing Social and Emotional Aspects of Learning (SEAL).* London: DCSF.

DCSF (2010) *Working Together to Safeguard Children: A Guide to Inter-Agency Working to Safeguard and Promote the Welfare of Children.* London: DCSF.

DCSF (2010a) *The use of force to control or restrain pupils: Guidance for schools in England.* London: DCSP

DfEE (1998) *Health and Safety of Pupils on Educational Visits: A Good Practice Guide.* London: DfEE.

DfEE (2000a) *Learning Journey* [3–7 and 7–11]. London: DfEE.

DfEE (2000b) *Learning Journey* [11–16]. London: DfEE.

DfES (2000) *Bullying: Don't Suffer in Silence – An Anti-Bullying Pack For Schools.* London: DfES.

DfES (2001) *The Special Educational Needs Code of Practice 2001.* London: HMSO.

DfES (2003) *Key Stage 3 National Strategy Advice on Whole School Behaviour and Attendance Policy.* London: DfES.

DfES (2004) *Every Child Matters: Change for Children.* London: DfES.

DfES (2005) *Primary National Strategy: KEEP – Key Elements of Effective Practice.* London: DfES.

DfES (2006) *What To Do If You're Worried a Child is Being Abused*. London: DfES.

DfES/DH (2005) *Managing Medicines in Schools and Early Years Settings*. London: DfES/Department of Health.

DH (1991) *The Children Act 1989 Guidance and regulations – Volume 2: Family Support, Day Care and Educational Provision for Young Children*. London: HMSO.

DH (2009) *Birth to Five: 2009 Edition*. London: Department of Health.

Donaldson, M. (1978) *Children's Minds*. London: Fontana.

Douch, P. (2004) 'What does inclusive play actually look like?' in *Playtoday*. Issue 42, May/June.

Drummond, M. et al (1984) *Making Assessment Work*. Swindon: NFER Nelson.

Dunn, K. et al (2003) *Developing Accessible Play Space: A Good Practice Guide*. London: ODPM.

Elliott, M. (2002) *Bullying: A Practical Guide to Coping for Schools*. 3rd edition. Harlow: Pearson Education in association with Kidscape.

Fontana, D. (1984) 'Personality and personal development' in D. Fontana (ed.) *The Education of the Young Child*. Oxford: Blackwell.

Foster-Cohen, S. (1999) *Introduction to Child Language Development*: Harlow: Longman.

Fox, G. (1998) *A Handbook for Learning Support Assistants*. London: David Fulton Publishers.

Griffin, S. (2008) *Inclusion, Equality and Diversity in Working with Children. London: Heinemann.*

Harding, J. and **Meldon-Smith**, L. (2001) *How to Make Observations and Assessments*. 2nd Edition. London: Hodder & Stoughton.

HSE (2004) *Getting to Grips with Manual Handling: A Short Guide*. Leaflet INDG143 (rev2) London: Health and Safety Executive Books.

HSE (2006) *Health and Safety Law: What You Should Know*. London: Health and Safety Executive Books.

HPA (2001) *Nutrition Matters for the Early Years: Guidance for Feeding Under Fives in the Childcare Setting*. Belfast: Health Promotion Agency.

Houghton, D. and **McColgan**, M. (1995) *Working With Children*. London: Collins Educational.

Hutchcroft, D. (1981) *Making Language Work*. London: McGraw-Hill.

ILAM (1999) *Indoor Play Areas: Guidance on Safe Practice*. Reading: Institute of Leisure and Amenity Management.

Johnstone, D. (2001) *An Introduction to Disability Studies*. London: David Fulton Publishers.

Kamen, T. (2000) *Psychology for Childhood Studies*. London: Hodder & Stoughton.

Kamen, T. (2004) *The Nanny Handbook*. London: Hodder & Stoughton.

Kamen, T. (2005) *The Playworker's Handbook*. London: Hodder Arnold.

Kamen, T. (2008) *Teaching Assistant's Handbook* 2nd edition. London: Hodder Arnold.

Kay, J. (2002) *Teaching Assistant's Handbook*. London: Continuum.

Kirby, P. et al (2003) *Building a Culture of Participation: Involving Children and Young People in Policy, Service Planning, Delivery and Evaluation – Handbook*. London: DfES.

Knowles, G. (2009) *Ensuring Every Child Matters*. London: Sage Publications.

Laing, A. and **Chazan**, M. (1984) 'Young children with special needs' (see **Fontana**, D.)

Leach, P (1994) *Children First*. London: Penguin.

Lee, V. and **Das Gupta**, P. (eds) (1995) *Children's Cognitive and Language Development*. Oxford: Blackwell.

Light, P. et al (ed) (1991) *Learning to Think*. London: Routledge.

Lindon, J. (1999) *Too Safe for Their own Good? Helping Children Learn about Risk and Lifeskills*. London: National Early Years Network.

Lindon (2002b) *What is Play?* Children's Play Information Service Factsheet. London: National Children's Bureau.

Lindon, J. (2007) *Understanding Children and Young People: Development from 5–18 years*. London: Hodder Arnold.

Lindon, J. (2008) *Safeguarding Children and Young People: Child Protection 0–18 years*. 3rd Edition. London: Hodder Education.

Matterson, E. (1989) *Play with a Purpose for the Under Sevens*. London: Penguin.

Meadows, S. (1993) *Child as Thinker: The Development of Cognition in Childhood*. London: Routledge.

Miller, L. (2002) *Observation Observed: An Outline of the Nature and Practice of Infant Observation*. London: Tavistock Clinic Foundation.

Moon, A. (1992) 'Take care of yourself' in *Child Education*, February issue. Leamington Spa: Scholastic.

Morris, J. and **Mort**, J. (1997) *Bright Ideas for the Early Years: Learning Through Play*. Leamington Spa: Scholastic.

Mulvaney, A. (1995) *Talking with Kids*. Sydney: Simon & Schuster.

Munn, P. et al (1992) *Effective Discipline in Secondary Schools and Classrooms*. London: Paul Chapman Publishing Ltd.

NDNA (2004) *National Occupational Standards in Children's Care, Learning and Development*. Brighouse: NDNA.

NPFA et al (2000) *Best Play: What Play Provision Should do for Children*. London: National Playing Fields Association.

O'Hagan, M. and **Smith**, M. (1994) *Special Issues in Child Care*. London: Bailliere Tindall.

Parsloe, E. (1999) *The Manager as Coach and Mentor*. London: Chartered Institute of Personnel & Development.

Petrie, P. (1997) *Communication with Children and Adults: Interpersonal Skills for Early Years and Play Work*. 2nd edition. London: Arnold.

Play Wales and PlayEducation (2001) *The First Claim: A Framework for Playwork Quality Assessment*. Cardiff: Play Wales.

QCA (2001) *Planning for Learning in the Foundation Stage*. London: Qualifications and Curriculum Authority.

QCA (2005) *ICT in the Foundation Stage*. London: Qualifications and Curriculum Authority.

RoSPA (2004a) *Play Safety Information Sheet: Information Sheet Number 16 – Legal Aspects of Safety on Children's Play Areas*. Birmingham: Royal Society for the Prevention of Accidents.

RoSPA (2004b) *Play Safety Information Sheet: Information Sheet Number 25 – Risk assessment of Children's Play Areas*. Birmingham: Royal Society for the Prevention of Accidents.

Sameroff, A. (1991) 'The social context of development' in M. Woodhead *et al* (eds) *Becoming a Person*. London: Routledge.

Scottish Executive (2006) *Nutritional Guidance for Early Years: Food Choices for Children Aged 1 – 5 Years in Early Education and Childcare Settings*. Scottish Executive.

Sirjai-Blatchford, I. (1994) *The Early Years: Laying the Foundations for Racial Equality*. Trentham Books.

SkillsActive (2004) *National Occupational Standards NVQ/SVQ Level 3 in Playwork*. London: SkillsActive.

Smart, C. (2001) *Special Educational Needs Policy*. Abbots Bromley: Special Educational Needs Press.

Steiner, B. et al (1993) *Profiling, Recording and Observing – A Resource Pack for the Early Years*. London: Routledge.

Street, C. (2002) The Benefits of Play. Highlight No.195. London: National Children's Bureau.

Taylor, J. (1973) *Reading and Writing in the First School*. London: George Allen and Unwin.

TDA (2006) *Primary Induction: Role and Context – For Teaching Assistant Trainers*. London: Training and Development Agency for Schools.

TDA (2007) *National Occupational Standards for Supporting Teaching and Learning In Schools*. London: Training and Development Agency for Schools.

Tharp and **Gallimore** (1991) 'A theory of teaching as assisted performance' (**Light**, P. 1991.)

Tobias, C. (1996) *The Way They Learn*. Colorado Springs: Focus on the Family Publishing.

Tough, J. (1976) *Listening to Children Talking*. London: Ward Lock Educational.

Tough, J. (1984) 'How young children develop and use language' in D. **Fontana** (ed.) *The Education of the Young Child*. Oxford: Blackwell.

Watkinson, A. (2003) *The Essential Guide for Competent Teaching Assistants*. London: David Fulton Publishers.

Whitehead, M. (1996) *The Development of Language and Literacy*. London: Hodder & Stoughton.

Wood, D. (1991) 'Aspects of teaching and learning' (see **Light**, P. 1991)

Wood, D. (1998) *How Children Think and Learn*. 2nd edition. Oxford: Blackwell Publishing.

Woodhead, M. (1991) 'Psychology and the cultural construction of children's needs' in M. **Woodhead** *et al* (ed) (1991) *Growing Up in a Changing Society*. London: Routledge.

Woolfson, R. (1991) *Children with Special Needs: A Guide for Parents and Carers*. London: Faber & Faber.

Yardley, A. (1984) 'Understanding and encouraging children's play' (see **Fontana**, D. 1984)

Index

Note: page numbers in **bold** refer to keyword definitions.